Psychovampires

Psychovampires

A Positive Approach to Energy Suckers

Hamid Peseschkian
Connie Voigt

Translated by

Tim Scott-Sandner

authorHOUSE®

AuthorHouse™ UK
1663 Liberty Drive
Bloomington, IN 47403 USA
www.authorhouse.co.uk
Phone: 0800.197.4150

Published by AuthorHouse 07/14/2015

ISBN: 978-1-5049-4471-7 (sc)
ISBN: 978-1-5049-4472-4 (e)

In love and gratitude
to the special people in my life.
It was you who helped me – despite the
Psychovampires – to keep my inner and outer smile.

Hamid Peseschkian

Dedicated to the psychovampires for their inspiration.
And to Peter Müller and Monique R. Siegel,
for your powerful synergy effects –
and special thanks to my dear British, American,
South African and Aussie friends
who have been waiting for the psychovampires
to come out in our universal language!

Connie Voigt

CONTENTS

PREFACE

My first real encounter with the phenomenon of psychovampires occurred in psychotherapy sessions with my patients & clients in the mid-1990s, who more often than not complained of being totally exhausted by people who rob them of their energy. I noticed that sometimes the mere thought of a certain person was enough to create this feeling of being drained and empty. This led to the creation of the term "psychovampires".

My experiences in seminars and training courses over the past ten years have only served to underline the fact that the suffering caused by psychovampires is universal and affects the well-being of (almost) everyone. I was dismayed to discover that some of these exhausting individuals pervaded my everyday life too, forcing me to come to terms with them one way or another.

As a practitioner of Positive Psychotherapy I was keen to mark out the positive aspects of the psychovampire phenomenon. With a touch of humour it's much easier to reflect on one's own being and not let oneself be affected and influenced by psychovampires. Each and every one of us has the power to control the psychovampires in our lives and live as we want to live. May you and those close to you benefit from the newly won energy.

Hamid Peseschkian, Wiesbaden/Germany, June 2015

***

As executive coach and specialist for communication, I have acquired a treasure-trove of stories from the working world. Without wishing to over-analyze these stories, it would seem that bullying is unfortunately a part of everyday life. One particular case of bullying close to home led me to ponder on the causes. Did I offer myself as a victim of bullying? Does the victim make it too easy for the bully? By establishing basic parameters for ourselves can we de-energize negative influences and divert them away from us. That's what this book is about.

Connie Voigt, Zurich & Berlin, June 2015

Half the thoughts and experiences in this book are taken from the lives and first-hand knowledge of the authors. We leave it to the imagination of our readers to decide which half.

Preface to the first English-language Edition

The story of Psychovampires has indeed been an international one:

The concept was perceived some twenty years ago while Hamid Peseschkian was working and travelling in Russia. Since then, it has been applied in numerous therapeutic sessions, seminars, workshops and lectures around the world by both authors.

During a meeting in Switzerland, the authors decided to write a book together; the original German-language edition was published by a Swiss publisher. This hard-copy version has been re-printed twice with an overall number of 6,000 copies.

In 2011, a pocket edition was published by the German publishing house Goldmann and is currently in the 4th edition with some further 6,000 copies.

Through psychotherapeutic colleagues of the World Association of Positive Psychotherapy (WAPP), the book has since then been published in Albanian (2010), Russian (2010), Lithuanian (2014) and Romanian language (2014). Turkish and other editions are planned. This reflects the multi-language and multi-cultural reality in Europe.

The authors are very happy that finally the English translation is available to the entire world community – we are very grateful to our translator Tim Scott-Sandner for this great job.

INTRODUCTION

Who or what is a psychovampire? How did this concept get its name? What does a psychovampire do to other people? Why is so important for each of us to recognize these energy suckers?

The term "Psychovampire" is a metaphoric concept intended to simplify our understanding of people who 'rob' us of energy. The term may seem flippant but it should still be taken seriously.

Everyone knows the feeling of a loss of emotional, spiritual, mental and physical energy after an encounter with another person. In daily life we don't bother to analyze this feeling any further although we do sense a draining of energy; we tend to accept the relations to those with whom we come into contact as unavoidable and accept many an irritation as part of the job. Some of us even blame ourselves for these negative sentiments. This is because we live in a time in which it is "in" to be under constant stress, indeed it's almost the done thing these days to be exhausted when you get home in the evening. This socially acceptable fatigue is really an act of self-deception. It underlies deep emotional stress which slowly builds up in our immediate social environment without our being fully aware of what is happening.

This book will assume that we are all surrounded by energy suckers or psychovampires capable of causing us emotional stress. There is no one typical vampire type; they come in all sorts of different guises. The authors have identified twelve psychovampire types: these are characterized in the first part of the book and presented in the form of true stories. Common to all encounters with vampire people is the imbalance between what we invest in energy and what we get in return. For some, the psychovampire is the boss, the project manager, the ex-partner, the team colleague, while for others it's the parents, husband or friends. In each of the cases described the psychological mechanism at the heart of the meeting with the respective vampire type is discussed in detail.

The second part of the book devotes itself to practical self-reflection. Chapter 4 deals with methods of exposing psychovampires in our immediate vicinity. Different strategies help to recognize potential vampires and vampire situations.

Chapter 5 takes a closer look at the psychological aspects. Why do we experience others as psychovampires? What are the reasons for our vulnerability? Psychovampires are good at re-opening the "victim's" old wounds, as a sort of catalyst. For their part the psychovampire "perpetrators" need the energy that comes from other people because they compensate their own deficits through those of others. The value of self-esteem plays a central role here because both perpetrators and victims lack self-esteem.

Chapter 6 takes us on a therapeutic excursion. On this trip, the Positive Psychotherapy method serves as a starting point for possible self-help. Preventive checks support a self-analysis offered to those who want to go more deeply into the subject matter. Pre-emptive measures and immunization techniques for contact with energy suckers are explained in Chapter 7. More practical check lists are available here too as an aid to reflection and in order to examine the phenomenon of reliance on others. The aim of every one of us is to lead a life based more or less on self-reliance.

Psychovampires are particularly adept at judging the right moment to attack their unsuspecting victim. In Chapter 8 we look at examples and tips to assist in a spontaneous disarmament maneuver. In the following Chapter 9 a series of psychovampire tests will help identify which signals a psychovampire picks up and interprets as an invitation to "attack". Inversely, we can discover if we ourselves have a psychovampire within us – assuming that the earlier chapters have not already awakened suspicions of our own vampirism! Any one of us can become a psychovampire in his environment - often without being aware of it or wanting it.

The higher aim of this book is to open the eyes of the victims and enable them to see psychovampires and then to suggest methods they can use to protect themselves – which involves accepting the basic premise that changing other people is (almost) impossible. Rendering psychovampires ineffective is in itself not easy but it is possible, and the solution lies in our own hands.

In this sense, this book is not primarily a compendium of guidelines for changing others, if only for the simple fact that this strategy is hardly likely to lead to success in the long run. It's more about the one person each of us can change the soonest – ourselves. In the end it's all down to admitting to ourselves that we give the psychovampire the power over us. Ultimately, it's our (unconscious) decision that lets a certain person have so much power over us. We must learn how to stand on our own in a professional or private relationship - full of self-determination and able to benefit from the positive effects.

PART 1

CHAPTER 1

The Psychovampire Phenomenon

A healthy person is not the one who has no problems but the one who takes a positive approach to them.
(from Positive Psychotherapy)

Does one of the following situations sound familiar? Or do you even live through something similar every day?

Situation 1:

Dr Florence (34) returns from her vacation fighting fit and looking forward to going back to her job in the clinic. She's recharged her batteries and is full of enthusiasm and energy as she resumes her work. On the ward she meets a nurse who greets her with the words: "Why are you smiling? Don't tell me you're glad to be back at work again?" In a matter of seconds this single negative remark has ruined any joy Florence had of being back at work. She feels drained, fed up and already looking forward to her next holiday.

Situation 2:

Chris (38) has an idea for a book he'd like to write and tells his girlfriend about it. Her immediate reaction is skeptical even though she doesn't know all the details: "There are books about that on the market already, yours is going to have to be really good and that will be difficult." To Chris this remark is not only dismissive, it's mind-shattering. His

3

girlfriend's lack of support fills him with a mixture of anger and disappointment. Her reaction totally deflates him. His girlfriend, on the other hand, is surprised at his behaviour ("You're always so sensitive. I'm only saying what I think. You're always saying I should be up front and honest.")

Situation 3:

Felicitas (24) studies psychology in a large city and visits her parents in the country one week-end. She's looking forward to telling them all about her life at university, what she's done and what she's learned about herself in the seminars. When she arrives it all spills out of her, or at least it would have, but her mother cuts her off in midstream: "You're looking very peaky and thin, dear. Are you eating properly in the city? What's the weather like up there?" No one's bothered about Felicitas' innermost thoughts and wishes. She has the feeling that her parents have no real interest in her and is devastated and angry with herself for opening up to them again, although she should have guessed it would happen.

How would you react if you were Florence, Chris or Felicitas? Let's take a look at what happened here. In all three cases the "victims" were demoralized by psychovampires without really being aware of the reason why. These are typical everyday situations dealing with what are, essentially, small matters. My reaction - strong or weak - depends on what the psychovampire, or his criticism, triggers in me as a person.

Just like these three people each one of us has their own vulnerable areas deep down inside which have crystallized in the course of our lives to become the sensitive spots they are today. We're normally unaware of them, or we believe we have long since solved the problem they represent. Psychovampires are somehow able to sense this vulnerability and press the right "button", which releases the same reaction every time – even years later. Trying to stop psychovampires pressing the button is useless, or impossible, if we haven't yet come to terms with this special weakness buried in our past. Our usual first reaction is to confront the psychovampire and defend ourselves so we talk to him and try to ward of the attack, as it were. Therapeutic experience shows, however, that this approach is hardly likely to lead to any lasting success. How am I supposed to prevent all the people I encounter every day from making their comments? In the end it's a matter of recognizing our own weak points, working on them, or at least learning to control them. Only then can we escape from our role as victims and become self-determined in our own right.

Why did the nurse, friend and parent psychovampires attack in this way? Did they do it at all consciously? How stable are they in their own lives? Are they notorious troublemakers and pessimists whose doubts determine their own existence? How self-determined are psychovampires and to what extent do the vampires' three victims allow their immediate environment to be controlled by other people? How can it be that psychovampires have such power over others and why do their victims let them take such control - unconsciously and unintentionally? How do potential victims recognise the tricks and techniques of psychovampires and how can they protect and "immunize" themselves against them long term?

A person who lets himself
be controlled by
someone else or
by entire situations
over a period of years,
pays for this later with a
basic discontent in life and
with increasing passivity.

Everybody strives to use and invest their energy in the required doses and lead a self-determined life. The psychovampire rules over the self-determination of others; he asserts an alien control over other people. A person who lets himself be controlled by someone else or even by entire situations over a period of years pays for this later with a basic dissatisfaction in life and with increasing apathy. In certain instances these situations can lead to depression and to a retreat from normal existence not to mention psychosomatic disorders and general fatigue.

Lasting release from the claws of psychovampires can come only from some deep introspection and a change in personal attitudes. Once we have recognised the psychological mechanisms in ourselves and our opponent, we can work out a practical strategy for getting rid of the psychovampire. If we make decisions without being clear about the mechanisms, the effect will only be brief and we'll be just as susceptible to the next psychovampire - who is bound to come our way. Our strategy should therefore focus not only – as so often – on the profiles of the "perpetrators", the psychovampires, but particularly on those of the victims. Once we've recognised the mechanism, we can work on ourselves – either as psychovampire or as victim.

CHAPTER 2

Psychovampire Types

"He who knows the goal can decide; he who decides finds tranquility; he who finds tranquility is sure; he who is sure can reflect; he who reflects can improve."

(Oriental proverb)

Psychovampires come in different guises. To make it easier to distinguish between the types, we've given them characterizing names and added a short profile of their victims. Psychovampires appear in both gender forms and in varying intensity. The descriptions are fully applicable to some while others show somewhat weaker symptoms of a certain type. Some people also fit into several categories. Someone who is perceived by one person as a vampire may find himself in the role of victim in his relationship with someone else. In short, everyone has the potential to be psychovampire and victim at the same time. Whether vampire or victim, they're mostly compensating for deficiencies in their own self-esteem. This idea is elaborated on in the therapeutic excursion in Chapter 6.

The Snare Vampire

This type grossly overestimates himself. He rarely allows contradiction, is unreasonable, despotic and regards himself as irreplaceable. Most of this breed are narcissists. Should the Snare Vampire happen to be a boss, he is likely to suck his co-workers dry while they, for their part, can never do anything right for him. They are the victims of his trap.

The "Yes, but..." Vampire

This psychovampire draws strength from his habit of beginning any reaction to ideas or general statements from others with the intro: "Yes, but... ". This basic position is experienced as negativistic and strenuous because the psychovampire then proceeds to roll off a variety of reasons why he cannot do or change something.

The Depressive Vampire

This one carries the burden of the whole world on his shoulders and commonly walks around with a look of intense suffering on his face. Everything is too difficult to him; in fact his whole existence is too much. He has loads of time at his disposal but barely manages to get anything done let alone restore any order to his life. He is also very self-centered and the basic principle of his existence is: "I'm having a hard time and I'm looking to you for moral support, inspiration, encouragement, joy in life, etc." He struggles through the day and infects everyone he meets with his own depressive mood.

The Monument Preservation Vampire

This guy wants nothing more than for the world to stand still. He guiding principle is: "We've always done it this way." He hates change and holds on fast to the old mantra: "If there'd been another good idea, I would have thought of it long ago." Times rarely change for Monument Preservation Vampire. His victims are creative people and colleagues with CEO potential who might just as well bang their heads against a brick wall with their innovations.

The Ice-box Vampire

Who hasn't experienced the scene where the "You-never-listen-to-me-when-I-have-a-problem" sobbing wife sits at the dinner table, while her husband, who's only been half-listening, suddenly decides it's time to take the dog for a walk. This emotionally cool vampire is very likely to be a well-respected figure in the world outside his home but at the relationship level he's more businesslike than intimate. He leaves his - usually very sensitive - victim out in the rain.

The Ignorant Vampire

The phenomenal thing about this fellow is that, although he may ask after your well-being, he's not particularly interested in an answer and leaves you, his victim, feeling thoroughly frustrated. The Ignorant Vampire makes a statement, calling for you to take a stand, express an opinion, but he's not really listening at all and soon turns away to talk to someone else instead. Potential victims of this species will be smitten with a feeling of emptiness and become convinced that they are dull and boring. They blame themselves for their failings.

The Himalaya Vampire

This vampire has set his sights high; he wants to scale the same peaks over and over again. Such ambition leads to suffocating expectations of those around him. It could be his own children or his co-workers - he unerringly demands results that are impossible to achieve. And if these goals should unexpectedly be reached, he dismisses them straight away. ("Anybody could have done that. It wasn't that difficult"). The Himalaya Vampire will completely ignore anyone who is unsuccessful. He denigrates others and even himself because he is always aiming higher and higher and yet never reaches his goal because he sets the bar a little higher every time. He is never inwardly satisfied and transmits this feeling of discontent to others.

The Polite Vampire

Too much politeness can also drain energy. Although this vampire wants to be a burden to nobody he ends up being a burden to everybody. His unfailing desire to help means that he constantly stretches himself to the limits and in doing so creates new problems for others. When, despite being a self-confessed non-IT person and ignoring a colleague's proffered advice, he buys himself a computer which is already out of date, he ultimately causes his colleague more work because he now has to exchange the model for a new one. If you invite the Polite Vampire to a restaurant and ask him what he'd like to drink, his usual reply will be: "What are you having? I don't mind what we drink." This procedure is repeated throughout the meal as the guest remains excruciatingly indecisive. The reserved nature of the psychovampire puts a great strain on those around him.

The Nosey Vampire

This species will poke his nose more or less everywhere where it doesn't belong. The urge to interfere in the affairs of others leads, even if for the most part unintentionally, to chaos and countless misunderstandings among the many unwitting victims he drags into what are basically trivial stories. The root cause of the Nosey Vampire's interference is a basic desire to create order. More often than not he achieves the exact opposite. And he usually gets off scot free as the unidentified person behind the scenes who was pulling the wires.

The Wolf In Sheep's Clothing Vampire

At first glance this character is friendly and unremarkable, but he's really a sly old fox. People are taken in by him over and over again. His pleasant and unassuming exterior is only a cover-up for something more sinister. To make matters worse, most of us don't recognise this type of psychovampire.

The It-Wasn't-Me Vampire

Examples of these vampires pervade the upper echelons of a company, they are the bosses who, after years of failed business strategies, are faced with the collapse of the enterprise and pin all blame on the staff. They "didn't work hard enough; if they had, the company would be still in a healthy condition." This vampire refuses to admit his own deficits: an inability to bear responsibility and retain control.

The Expert Vampire

Someone who has no idea but regards himself as an expert. He has an answer for every difficult situation, is a know-all and offends and exasperates others with his ill-considered advice. The Expert Psychovampire devours his victim's time by expanding endlessly on his supposed knowledge and woe betide anyone who dares to suggest that he has no idea what he's talking about – they risk a permanently fraught relationship with him in future.

Do some of these situations ring a bell? As a victim or a vampire? If they do, read on (if not, then read on anyway). We want to show you how, as a potential victim, you can create an impervious shield to protect you long-term from the various psychovampire types. You will change your behaviour so that the vampire stops seeing you as a possible victim, or he will at least lose his power over you, although he himself will not have changed his behaviour one bit. If, on the other hand, you have unmasked yourself as a psychovampire, it's just as advisable to read on and understand how others you see and why certain situations are not at all what you may have perceived them to be at first glance.

Exactly how a psychovampire pinpoints the soft areas of his potential victims remains a mystery in spite of extensive psychological research. The mechanisms are comparable with the phenomenon of love at first sight, which makes it all the more dangerous in the hands of vampires. In the end it's up to the victims to change the situation by doing some ground work on themselves.

Paradoxically, psychovampires are almost always to be found in the victim's immediate surroundings. They are very close to the emotional world of their prey, either as direct superiors at work or as a family member at home. This explains their easy access to the hearts and weaker points of their respective victims. And because the vampire is so close to us in this way we tend to react with excessive sensitivity to actions or statements which in normal circumstances, and at a greater distance, we would not have taken so personally. At the same time it makes dealing with psychovampires so difficult because, in most cases, you can't just fire them and completely avoid their company. Nor it is reasonable to dismiss your partner, the children, the boss, the mother-in-law or the neighbor. So the only solution is to build up your own self-defense mechanisms.

The allegory of the psychovampire helps to create a positive perception of what is, in fact, an imbalance in interpersonal relationships. One could say that psychovampires provide us with a quick and free course in self-awareness, a short analysis which in therapy terms could take several years, though unfortunately we didn't ask them for it. When reading the following case studies, which are taken from the lives and experiences of the authors, you will come to better understand many of the situations you have experienced over the years but perhaps were never able to analyze or evaluate properly.

CHAPTER 3

Stories of common vampire types

Theory and practice of understanding human nature

A receptive young man blessed with a thirst for knowledge and wisdom had studied physiognomy, the science of physical expression, in Egypt, under great privation and far from his native country. His studies lasted six years at the end of which he took his exam and passed with honours. Filled with joy and pride he set off back to his homeland. On the way he observed everybody he met through the eyes of his newly won knowledge and, wishing to increase this, paid particular attention to their facial expressions.

One day he met a man in whose face he recognized six distinctive qualities: envy, jealousy, greed, avarice, miserliness and ruthlessness. "My God, what an amazing physiognomy, I've never seen or heard of such a thing. This is a chance to put my theory to the test." While these thoughts were going through his head, the stranger approached him. He had a friendly, gentle and modest disposition: "Oh master! The day is almost over and the next village is such a long way off. My hut is small and dark but I will look after you well. What an honor it would be for me if I might call you my guest tonight and how happy your presence would make me!" Our astonished traveler thought: "How remarkable! What a difference exists between the utterances of this stranger and his hideous expression."

Deeply shocked by this realization, he began to doubt his studies of the last six years. To be more certain, he accepted the stranger's invitation. His host spoilt him with tea, coffee, juice, sweetmeats and a waterpipe. He showered his guest with kindness, attention, generosity and courtesy and succeeded in making our traveler prolong his stay for three days and nights. Finally, the scholar managed to overcome the effusive hospitality and seized the moment to continue his journey.

When the time came to say good-bye, his host handed him an envelope with the words: "Great sir! This is your bill." "What bill?" asked the surprised scholar. Like a sword drawn from its scabbard, his host suddenly revealed his true face. Frowning menacingly he shouted in an angry voice: "Such impertinence! What were you thinking as you sat there eating all my food? Did you think that everything was for free?" These words brought the scholar to his senses with a jolt and he opened the letter in silence. He saw that what he had eaten, and had not eaten, had been charged a hundred fold. He wasn't even able to pay half the sum demanded. Out of necessity he dismounted from his horse and gave it to his host in addition to the saddle and all his belongings and when this did not suffice he took off his traveling clothes and set off on foot. As if in raptures, he walked with the upper part of the body bowing with every step he took along the way and his voice could still be heard from a long way off as he muttered to himself: "Thank God, thank God that my six years of study were not in vain!" (from 'Abdu'l-Bahá) *

*from: Nossrat Peseschkian „Oriental Stories as Tools in Psychotherapy – The Merchant and the Parrot." Springer Heidelberg Berlin New York, 1986 (German original: Der Kaufmann und der Papagei; Fischer Taschenbuch Verlag, Bd.3300, S 137/38,- Copyright © S. Fischer Verlag GmbH, Frankfurt am Main, 1979)

In the following case studies we explain the "methods" used by the different psychovampire types to compensate for their own deficits and how the individual victims react to their "attacks". What the victims for their part have in common is a predictably low self-esteem which may be of a temporary nature or a permanent condition and which makes them a ready target for vampires who single them out and hone in on them as if by instinct. This gut feeling and their initial verbal reaction is what helps vampires "identify" potential victims. They send out signals which the psychovampire picks up on his invisible antenna and once he's locked on the victim's fate is all but sealed.

We also have to distinguish between psychovampires who are a constant feature in a person's life and therefore able to drain the energy of those close to them on a regular basis and those vampires who only "go for the throat" in incidental attacks on people whose self-confidence may be temporarily weakened (as in the cases of Doctor Florence and the author Chris).

The Snare Vampire

When the boss strangles his employees

We've all had the bad luck to experience this type at some point in our careers: the despot disguised as our boss. He - or maybe also she - is egocentric, totally overestimates himself (we'll stay with "he" because there are still very few women at executive level), rarely allows any contradiction, knows everything better and regards himself as irreplaceable. Once he's sensed a victim, he puts an invisible rope around his unfortunate neck and uses him to give vent to a repressed desire for recognition and the need to get his own work done first. His unsuspecting victims don't feel the rope at first; it's only later that he begins to choke.

Example:

The boss enters the office of his finance manager without knocking on the door and tells him he urgently requires a complete run-down of the finances for his presentation to the board of directors – in two days' time. "This has absolute priority", he adds. As a man of conscience, the finance manager puts his own important projects on the back burner and begins on the work for his boss. A few hours later his boss storms into his office again demanding to know how the other projects are going. The finance manager is at pains to point out that he's now working on the urgent project (run-down of the finances for his boss), to which his boss replies with some disdain in his voice: "A man in your position should be able to do several jobs at the same time." The manager is duly downcast by all this and his good mood is spoiled for the rest of the day. His first reaction is anger but he keeps it to himself. With situations like this recurring every single day the medium term effects on the manager take the form of psychosomatic disorders (stomach cramps) and demotivation. His thoughts turn increasingly to quitting his job and going to work somewhere else.

The Perpetrator Profile:

The Snare Vampire comes in two different categories: the first is a narcissistic person who firmly believes that his affairs are of greater relevance than those of his fellow men. This vampire shows a total lack of empathy in the emotional world and his experiences with other people, while at the same time he's hypersensitive to criticism from others. Rage and disdain are his reactions to adverse comment from his peers.

Very often this vampire type is at the mercy of his need for instant gratification of certain urges. In children it's seen as perfectly normal (up to a certain age) when they demand to have a need or a wish fulfilled immediately: "I want a drink now." "I have to go on the toilet now." "I can't wait five minutes." This behaviour is, sadly, also prevalent among certain adults: the boss who summons his employee to the office because he wants something done immediately although he could discuss the same matter with the employee at the meeting due to take place in the next hour; or the person who's annoyed when someone doesn't answer their cell phone straightaway just because they have to speak to them – now! Such unsolicited behaviour puts victims under even more pressure.

The Victim Profile

Victims of the Snare Vampire frequently need a lot of recognition from outside and seek the reasons for failure in themselves. They constantly strive to please the Snare Vampire and, like the vampire who ensnares them, they too suffer from low self-esteem. They often idealize the vampire because they fail to recognise that the psychovampire himself suffers from a lack of self-confidence.

The psychological mechanism:

For the oppressor, in this case the boss, nothing happens fast enough. You can't win; no matter what you do, he's going to put that rope around your neck. People who come into contact with the Snare Vampire are victims of his fundamental distrust in the abilities of others, which in itself is an indication of the psychovampire's low self-esteem. He must put people down in order to feel better himself. A good image to illustrate this is a seesaw, the sort you find in playgrounds: if I push the person at the other end down, I go to the top of my end. By downgrading others I raise my own self-esteem. Unfortunately, this effect does not last for long. Since there's no rational reason for mistrusting the abilities of his fellow men, the Snare Vampire can reasonably be accused of delusional behaviour - he relates everything to himself and interprets actions as hostile and directed against him as a person.

Life partners set a snare for each other

Snare Vampires enjoy meeting each other in a private context and are frequently drawn together through their like-minded verbal exchanges. They present a mutual challenge which can be extremely explosive at the beginning - and highly erotic. However, once the fronts are clear, the struggle for power begins. From the psychological angle it's worth pointing out that almost all interpersonal problems can be reduced to three factors: love, power and money. Power also plays a particularly important role in the following example and this makes it the determining factor.

Example:

Steven W. and Stephanie B. have lived together for nine years. In the last two years though their relationship has deteriorated to become a marriage of convenience based on purely professional criteria. Both are successful and feisty individuals; neither realizes that the reason for their staying together is rooted in a craving for mutual attention and the dream of unending success. They see their problems as something unique which can only be understood by certain people - themselves. The inner pressure to receive recognition is incomparably higher than it is in other people because of their constant striving for more power. They rely on each other for the attention and admiration they crave, dishing up success stories for their mutual benefit. But at the same time they're also comparing their success rates; they are after all in close competition with each other. They're plagued by strong feelings of envy. Steven will tell his lover Sandra Z. that he earns much more money than Stephanie, even though she's more in the limelight than he is. "In my job as consultant I have much more elbowroom and possibilities", says Steven with considerable arrogance.

Victim and perpetrator profile:

Both are competitive, i.e. purely target- and result-oriented; their self-evaluation is exaggerated and they are keen to measure themselves with equally strong people and compete with each other.

The psychological mechanism:

Both vampires have a low self-esteem which they fail to recognise in themselves. This makes them both perpetrators of the struggle for power as well as victims of the snares they set for each other. They drain each other in equal measures.

Antidote to Snare Vampires:

Once you have become aware that your opposite number is a narcissist, i.e. someone who can never get enough praise and recognition and for whom you can never do things right, just leave it at that. Reflect on your core strengths and abilities and simply stick to your agenda without letting yourself be distracted.

The "Yes, but..." Vampire

Work colleagues grind away at the boss's nerves

Imagine you're a project manager and responsible for a team of 20 people. You're just about launch a new project and are bursting with energy and motivation and then find out that two co-workers are not pulling their weight. As a rationally thinking, success-oriented project manager you fail to see where the problem lies; you've taken them through the concept in great detail from A to Z and now you're at a loss to figure out why the two of them are constantly expressing doubts about their role and the entire project.

Conversation examples:

Project manager to employee 1: "Mr. J., I think you should take sole responsibility for IT. You have enough experience by now and, besides, you've earned promotion."

Mr. J.: «Yes, but I don't have much idea about Support. What am I supposed to do when something goes wrong? And apart from that, I think there are too many risks involved in this project."

Obviously the project manager has overestimated this colleague by failing to take his emotional state into account.

He also has to solve the problem of his new assistant whose predecessor has already left the company, which means there's no one to show her the ropes.

Project manager to employee 2: "Ms. A., I appreciate that you're new on the team but I don't think you have to check every little detail with me. This takes up too much of my time and, besides, your tasks are not so complicated that you can't solve problems independently."

Mrs. A.: "Yes, but as a new employee I need to ask about everything and check back with you. This all takes a little longer at first and that's why you should agree to overtime."

The project manager hasn't budgeted for any overtime and doesn't see why he should. Whenever he sees Ms. A.; she gives him the impression of being overworked and tired out. A few minutes into a conversation with her and he feels sucked dry and finds himself struggling to keep his buoyant mood going. Extra perks and uplifting praise only have a short-term effect on Ms. A.; she quickly reverts to her familiar attitude of recrimination and accusation. The project manager had initially invested a lot of energy in Ms. A.; he was keen that she should get on-the-job training and settle in well, but her constant insecurity – prefaced by the words "Yes, but..." are not only making him aggressive, but helpless too.

Perpetrator profile Mr. J.

Where other people see possibilities and opportunities, our "Yes, but..." Psychovampire only sees problems and he's quick to doubt his own abilities even before any project gets going. He refuses promotion because it would mean living up to greater expectations and having to take on new responsibilities. He's the classic "grey mouse". He leaves it to others to make the most important decisions and always endorses the actions of others – although they may be in the wrong – for fear of being rejected. His permanent fear and insecurity bring out the worst in success-oriented people like his superiors.

Perpetrator profile Ms. A.

This "Yes, but..." Psychovampire is equally indecisive and weak-willed, doesn't trust her own judgment and notoriously seeks advice from her peers. She has a tendency to agree too easily to what others propose and will always follow the path of least resistance, like a flag in the wind, lacking any sort of initiative and incapable of acting alone. This commonly manifests itself verbally in such remarks as "What shall I do? How long is the settling-in period? Who is my contact if I have any questions?" She needs large and regular slices of praise und ego-boosting, looks and often feels helpless, makes a lot of mistakes, is unmotivated, dependent and easily daunted by criticism or rejection.

Victim profile:

Victims are goal- and success-oriented people used to tackling problems and issues and getting results and they expect this from others too ("go-getter type"). No task is too great from them or too impossible; they're ambitious enough to want to master every challenge and this often means putting themselves under a lot of stress – stress that is intensified by decelerators like the "Yes, but..." Vampires. This go-getter can also come across to some as a psychovampire; he's very target-oriented and doesn't give way to personal weaknesses, etc., and his relationship potential is seldom promising. This doer frequently reaches his limits when it comes to staff management responsibilities and finds that his goal-oriented approach falls on deaf ears and that he has no strategy for coping at the communication level.

The psychological mechanism:

The under-developed self-esteem of the "Yes, but..." Vampires releases a caring urge in the victim. It's a bit like being a holiday entertainer whose job is to motivate, encourage and generally get things moving. Since the victim already has his hands full tackling the job or jobs in hand, coaxing the reticent "Yes, but..." Vampires is likely to be seen as tiresome and an additional stress factor which he could really do without.

Antidote for "Yes, but..." Vampires:

In this context the saying "discretion is the better part of valor" makes plenty of sense. When confronted with "Yes, but..." Vampires, we use up an incredibly large amount of energy falling into the same trap over and over again by imagining that we can change the other person by uttering some clever words of encouragement. Sometimes you keep trying in vain for years or even decades. The best thing you can do is give up, but without being offended. Decide consciously that you're no longer prepared to sacrifice your energy for somebody who does not deserve it.

Refuse to be drawn into the "Yes, but..." discussion and present the psychovampire with a fait accompli using statements like "That's the way it is", "Thanks for your input but we will keep to the original plan", or simply "Thanks". And then push your scheme through.

The Depressive Vampire

The depressive office worker type as boss

This prototype may carry the weight of the world on his shoulders, as the old saying goes, but he himself spends a lot of time resting on the shoulders of his peers - and he does so with such gravitational force that he soon becomes "unbearable" in the truest sense of the word.

Colleagues like this can normally be heard sighing out loud even though their desk isn't exactly weighed down with work. The slightest thing irritates them: it could be the woman who passes by on her way to the photocopier and shouts a friendly "Hello", or the guy who can't get rid of his cough and has been the main cause of raised noise levels in the open-plan office for some months now.

People are never sure if the Depressive Vampire is in a permanently bad mood or if bad things keep happening to him, or if he's simply the moody type. His take is that the others are always to blame. Like the colleague who dashes past on her way to the copier. Can't she see that he doesn't want to be disturbed in his misery, isn't it plain enough to everybody? In actual fact, it isn't, but because the Depressive Psychovampire assumes it is, he believes that everything that happens around him which he doesn't agree with must be directed against him; in other words, he's convinced that his female colleague is out to annoy him and deliberately takes the short cut for that reason. In his depressive state the Depressive Psychovampire reveals himself as massively egocentric.

Having a depressive vampire as boss is hardly conducive to easing the load. Here's a tale from a publishing house:

Monk has been editor-in-chief of a business magazine for three years. He oversees two people one of whom was already there when he took over the job. This is Astrid, an employee he hasn't liked from the start. The two of them keep communication to a minimum, partly because they have little to say to each other and partly because they tend to get hold of the wrong stick whenever they do talk - a combination which doen't exactly contribute to a happy working atmosphere, though neither is willing to take any appropriate action. Monk and Astrid maintain an icy silence and so would they have continued if Monk hadn't finally taken the decision, during an trip to Asia, to fire his colleague.

But the "silly cow", as he calls her when speaking to other publishing colleagues, has an trump card up her sleeve to thwart this macho: while he's away she officially informs the company that she's pregnant. Monk - back from his vacation - is baffled. He strongly suspects that her pregancny has somethnig to do with him. "She chose this moment to become pregant because she knows that I was about to fire her and now she thinks she can keep her job", he complains to his other female colleague. She can't believe her ears. How can a boss think that his employee would be willing to change her life and stop taking the usual precautions just because of him?

Monk is obviously suffering from what is known in layman's terms as paranoia. Co-workers only have to make an innocent inquiry about where he spends his two-hour lunchbreaks for him to retort that this is his own business. It wouldn't be so bad if he came back in a happy mood, but the time spent out of the office never seems to cheer him up. He never smiles, either before or after the long break. He can roar with laughter at a good joke but a smile seldom strays across his face.

Characters like Monk are extremely damaging to team spirit because the fear that others might do something to them often drives them to act pre-emptively and talk about people behind their backs. They do this on the supposition that someone else would otherwise do it. To compensate for their seriously dented self-confidence many a Depressive Psychovampire adopts an arrogant stance - if they haven't already had that effect on others. Although Monk tries to hide his frustration under a certain arrogance (which he always denies), he always misses out because his macho-like behaviour aggravates the situation, especially among his female colleagues. This a especially apparent at meetings and social gatherings where he strikes a high profile. He interferes in other people affairs and talks them down if he feels they might be competition - you could also say he does it when he senses that somebody else might be better. It goes without saying that Monk has issues with career women. They diminish the influence he has laboriously built up. He regards successful colleagues and above all female colleagues with hidden envy, something they themselves have difficulty relating to because they only see his arrogant facade. And so this psychovampire with his bundle of frustration, fear and envy continues to drain the energy of entire teams and, to cap it all, is surprised when their motivation starts to dwindle. Monk would never dream of thinking that he might be responsible for this drop in motivation. Caught in his negative mindset, problems are always the fault of others. This pushes Monk into the additional category of the "It Wasn't Me" Vampire. Whenever things in Production or IT go slightly wrong, Monk lacks the strength of mind to admit his own mistakes simply because he isn't able to recognise them as his. He could be taking on responsibility for others and for the team but he's far too occupied with himself. Monk is caught in the vice-like grip of his own deficiencies. To free himself from this stranglehold he would first need to engage in some healthy self-reflection.

The depressive entrepreneur type

"Whenever the boss is away, it's like being on a health farm", is how the workers in a medium-sized company in London see their CEO. If the boss isn't there the staff can get on with their work in peace and quiet. "Have you got a moment?" is the stressed call they're otherwise used to hearing from his office, several times a day. This request has serious consequences for the whole staff: they're all dragged from their work, lose their concentration and are made to feel like servants at the beck and call of their master. As it that wasn't enough, his reasons for panicking are even more questionable. He can't resist telling everyone about all the negative news, whether it's a contract that didn't work out or advice from the company consultants, which he generally assesses negatively. Praise or recognition are luxuries for his employees and it's a luxury they seldom enjoy. It's no wonder then that the fluctuation rate is exceptionally high among the workforce. "No sooner has a new worker started here than the boss had something negative to say about him. We assumed that he made negative comments about all of us." says a former employee. Defamation of character is unlikely to contribute to a good working atmosphere; team cohesion has no chance to develop, not only because the new personnel are never there long enough to get old, but also because nobody can trust anyone else.

Simon, a former employee, recalls some sales talks between himself, his boss and a potential American client: "Jeff Goldstein who's a Harvard professor in addition to owning a business asked me as a new employee in the round which challenges I faced in my private life. I found the question unusual but exciting because it signalled the interest of this possible customer and also showed that we were getting on", says Simon. Just three days later his boss mentioned this conversation with Golstein to him after the order had gone to a bigger rival firm. He was extremely annoyed about this setback, as he called it. He was more than convinced that it was Simon's fault although he didn't say so directly. Instead he stalked Simon with questions about the possible reasons. He let him feel in not so many words that he was the guilty party. When Simon asked him face to face if he held him responsible for the lost contract his boss replied in a tone intended to appease: "No, no."

For Simon however, the situation was quite clear: the bigger competitor had more experience with international orders and that's why it won the order.

In the course of time, the thought patterns of the boss, "It's everyone else's fault ", took on an even darker hue: "Everything's bad" and "Everyone's useless", as Simon was disappointed to observe. In front of the entrance to the managing director's office there stood a lifesize sculpture of a black vulture with a matt black patina. It seemed to possess some special symbolic power. "This vulture had a detrimental effect on everybody; every second person tripped over it on their way to the boss's office. It gave me the creeps everytime; it just got worse and worse", Simon still remembers it vividly to this day. "This creature was uncanny, there was something dark and inaccessible about it, just like the boss".

This Depressive Psychovampire boss, once a leading icon in his field, lacked the necessary charm and sense of humour. His sales figures decreased by about 50 percent and this although his branch was booming. Company forecasts were all negative too. The reasons for his depression were not fully apparent to his team. Simon conjectured that his boss, now in his sixties, wanted to hand over the reins to someone else but couldn't bring himself to do it and, as a result of this inability to let go, had developed destructive behaviour patterns. He would frequently storm out of meetings, white with anger, muttering, "I can't to listen to this any longer", although as far as his staff were concerned there was really no occasion for such a fit of rage, or behaviour that was, ultimately, bad for business. To all intents and purposes it looked as though he was subconsciously destroying everything he had successfully built up in his best years, just because his ego wouldn't allow him to let others participate in his success and continue it.

Perpetrator profile:

There are many reasons why people run the risk of falling into a state of depression, some only in short phases, others in a long, drawn out process. The great danger here is the gradual development which keeps the disorder under wraps until it's already taken a real hold. The fatal dilemma for Depressive Psychovampires is that their immediate environment - their victims – don't recognize the depression. Victims only see the painted facade of arrogance through which frustration always shines. Their fears - if any - are confirmed much later when the team is no longer efficent and other victims have long since laid down their weapons and given up, either for reasons of self-protection or because of their own frustration.

Victim profile:

It's not easy for anybody to avoid a bad mood. No other psychovampire is immune against the depressive. He spoils the fun, no matter where he is and that makes the reviving antidote all the more important.

Antidote for the depressive vampire:

Why not try an analysis? Ask yourself what motivates the vampire; why is he in a bad temper? It's not difficult to get close to these vampires and find out things about them; they feel flattered and wanted, which in turn increases their self-confidence. Even if these encounters take a lot of willpower, because the chances are that the vampire talks badly about you too, try to ignore your own anger towards him. If you approach him with care, you will win his trust and may just be able to help him. This would be the best antidote, one which is earned through great effort and energy but which is also the most effective formula for rendering this type harmless, for others and, ultimately, for yourself.

The Monument Preservation Vampire

Parental monument preservation with symptoms of paralysis

Example:

"Tanya, we know you always do what you want anyway but if we had the chance we wouldn't go abroad for a year", says Martha, her mother, adopting her familar reproachful, concerned face. Tanya is irritated, as she is whenever she sees this face. She feels caught between two stools and fears a big family argument if she goes through with her plan. Her father, Victor, presents her with an ultimatum: "If you go ahead with the year in France I won't talk to you any more". Like most teenagers Tanya hovers between giving way to her parents and therefore allowing other people to control her life - a frequnet dilemma in childhood and early youth - and the growing desire to take her life into her own hands and become independent.

Perpetrator profile:

Parents who can't subdue the urge to pass their own ideas of good, old, tried and tested values on to their children belong for the most part to the generation that rebuilt society after the Second World War. Their own childhood was marked by the fear of war - even at 70 years of age many have not been able to forget the air-raids and the vision of whole cities lying in ruins. Their need for security is understandably much greater. In psychotherapy terms this manifests itself in activities such as house purchase, building a house, financial security, inheritance, fear of job changes and the lack of courage to take a risk and try something different. No wonder then that the same parents fail to comprehend the next - untraumatized - generation which has not developed the same habit of thinking in terms of security and is more open for experimenting in life or taking time out career-wise.

Victim profile:

Teenagers who are forced to bend to the will of their parents often feel that their lives are not under their control. The real question is whether they're able to break the mould later in life and learn to stand on their own two feet and make their own decisions. Some never quite manage it. They're caught in a paradigm for which their own parents must bear the full blame (if unintentionally). This uncertainty about what is best plagues them as adults later on when making decisions becomes a nightmare - from little things like buying clothes to major decisions like moving or marriage. These people always need approval from their peers before they can decide on anything.

The psychological mechanism:

The Monument Preservation Vampire is averse to change; he clings to proven traditions and processes and tries to force others to come round to his way of thinking, even if - as in the extreme case of Tanya's father - this means issuing threats. Early victims are paralyzed by this ritualized blackmail and become "safety first" fanatics in adult life. As small children and later as adolescents they're prevented from making their own experiences, constantly being warned by over-protective parents, "Don't do that, something might happen to you". This begins in the sandpit, carries on through the first bike and then into relationships, "be careful, or you'll be sorry when she leaves you". Such people not only suffer from low self-esteem, they belong to the so-called dependent or under-confident personalities. Their uppermost worry is to make sure that nothing can go wrong and that everyone agrees, only then are they willing to take action. Creativity, spontaneity and innovation never get a look in.

The dead duck succession plan

Example:

71-year-old Fritz K. built up a successful family business in the Sixties. He began with the kind of small loan that wouldn't get him very far if he was setting up a company today. His oldest son, Roman (45), works his way up the company ladder and naturally expects to succeed his father one day. After two years of working together he has what it needs to take over the reins but the father has no intention of letting go, let alone retiring. "I've decided to carry on working here until I'm 90", he announces to Roman one morning. "As long I can still breathe, I'll make all the decisions here", he adds. Roman's father starts to make little mistakes; they happen more and more frequently and before long the first customer complaints start rolling in. Ignoring the obvious, his father refuses to pass the baton to his son. The inevitable happens, there's a big confrontation which ends in his son threatening to leave the company. Over and over again his father repeats the same old mantras, "I built all this up and you want to take over, just like that". Every new idea his son presents is met with, "we've already tried that" or "we used to do it differently in the old days and the customers were always satisfied".

Perpetrator profile:

Individuals like Fritz K. have narcissistic personalities and are oblivious to the rapid social progress going on around them. They can't let go and, even worse, are normally very headstrong. They live in a sort of cocoon in which their victims are trapped with them. Such phenomena occur all too frequently in family businesses. These psychovampires don't notice that other people are making fun of them and not taking them seriously. And so they carry on blindly destroying everything they've built up over the years, until the time comes when they're written off as senile or physically removed from power. Some will agree to a successor as long as he or she tows the line and lets the old man continue to pull the strings. This is common practice in multinational concerns where, for example, the chairman of the board is given a position on the board of directors. Whatever the course of action, conflict is programmed: if the successor is better, the outgoing boss is insulted; if he's worse, the old boy feels justified in his assertion that no one can do the job better than himself and that he should have stayed on longer as boss.

Victim profile:

Victims are typically forward-thinking, innovative people with a talent for calculated risks. They're often assumed to be hostile to traditional values, though this is seldom true. As new CEO they would expect to enjoy the same freedoms as their predecessor did in his pioneering days and while they may not be as charismatic as their predecessor they do strive to impress through hard work, performance and know-how. Unless they're given full responsibility to steer company policy they gradually lose their initial impetus, especially when their ideas are being constantly blocked from above. It's all to easy to take these setbacks as personal and this can have a destructive and lasting effect if the situation continues over a long period of time.

The psychological mechanism:

The risk-shy person meets the risk-taker. Once he was willing to take the odd risk in his youth, now the Monument Preservation Vampire is generally averse to risk and doesn't see how important it is for the continued growth of the company to review the situation at regular intervals, take new risks where necessary and adapt products or services to changing customer needs. Being a narcissist, the Monument Preservation Vampire cannot tolerate any other king in his place, which is why he sees every potential successor as an insult and a menace. We can often observe this phenomenon in heads of state who should have resigned long ago but manage to somehow find a reason to stay on in power or, when that fails, simply change the constitution to win themselves another term of office. And when it does finally come to the inevitable crunch they make sure that their successsor is such a weak-willed person that the people are soon regretting his removal, or so that they can say to themselves, "You see, I knew I was better". The narcissist has low self-esteem but is paradoxically seen by others as very strong-willed. Like a king with his courtiers, he needs an audience. Once the audience is gone - in our example, the job or the high position - not much remains of his self-esteem.

When the new boss is at the mercy of a horde of Monument Preservation Vampires

Monument Preservation Vampires need not be old by definition, as in the two previous examples. Younger people can also be inherently averse to change.

Example:

When Anthony S. took on his new job as bank manager, he was given the task of restructuring the organisation. It didn't take long before he realized that the staff were totally uncooperative and blocking any innovative ideas - even when these made sense and contributed to the general well-being of the whole team. Time and again he was forced to hear statements like "we've always done it this way, why we should change it now?".

Perpetrator profile:

These phlegmatic types put up great resistance when their "comfort zone" is threatened. They're the types who have arrived at exactly 8 o'clock in the morning for the last 20 years, unpacked their briefcase and left the office again at 4.30 on the dot every afternoon. In their minds they're settled for life and virtually unsackable - a sad fact confirmed by their contracts. And if I'm unsackable why should I should change and move up the career ladder?

Interestingly enough, this process can also be observed in countless partnerships. Without wanting to pass judgement we like to call these "public sector employee marriages". Once I've said "Yes" and signed the marriage contract, the other person has to take me as I am.

Victim profile:

Weak leadership is characterized by a tendency to want to please everyone – a personality trait which is doomed to failure when you come up against hordes of Monument Preservation Vampires. As a boss they don't get very far with innovation, in extreme cases they suffer regular harassment at the hands of their colleagues and often lose their new job. Some go voluntarily after the apathy and unfriendly atmosphere has worn them down, others are regarded by the management as not being up to the responsibilty and soon shown the door.

Antidote for Monument Preservation Vampires:

Accept the fact that everything you do or not do is going to upset somebody. This may be for no other reason than that you exist. Your presence, your very existence, as younger successor, for example, or your success, is sufficient to attract the hostility of your peers. As an antidote, try to reduce the points of contact to a minimum, because the sad fact is that conflicts are inevitable. You have to live with the knowledge that there's no way you are going to avoid offending someone so set in their ways. They're the only ones in the world who can get themselves out of that situation - at least theoretically. The only problem is that such people are unlikely to want or even be able to adapt to new situations and will regard them as a threat. In such difficult cases it can make sense for you to look around for a new field of activity for your talents, because if you don't the psychovampire will make your life hell. Give yourself, the vampire and the situation, a deadline of about two years. If the circumstances haven't improved by that time, clear your desk and leave - not with a grudge but full of self-confidence and your head held high.

The Ice-box Vampire

When a cold wind blows from the boss's office

Gary K. was a successful CEO in an international company. Over the years his colleagues had come to respect his clear mind, but they also knew how unapproachable and, for no apparent reason, how hostile he could be. When in-house attorney Robert W. stepped into Gary's office one day he wished he could have turned right round and gone back out again: Gary K. looked at him as if they were perfect strangers. Robert W. had obviously chosen the wrong moment to request a meeting but he needed the CEO's decision on an urgent matter that could have a beneficial outcome on the future of the whole company. Robert W. was non-plussed. Whenever his boss had appointments with customers outside the company he always observed how courteous and charming his boss could be to corporate clients. One thing was clear: Gary K.'s friendliness was carefully measured to suit the occasion.

Two classics from the living-room

Dialogues in private homes:

Olivia (32) and Jared (33) are sitting together one evening. Jared's talking about his day at the office. He's completely swamped with work, there's a lot of bad feeling all round and talk of reduncancies. Olivia listens for a while and then cuts him off in midstream: "What shall we cook for dinner tomorrow?" Jared's annoyed and complains that she never listens to him. She replies: "What's up with you? I was listening to what you were saying but I still have to plan the shopping tomorrow."

Susan (32) and Keith (36) have lived together for seven years. Susan's been thinking a lot about her life lately and their relationship. In the evening they have a longer discussion about their life together and the future. Keith, not one for expressing his feelings too openly, declares over dinner that things can't go on the way they are. He feels that she's gradually moving away from him, they don't seem to have anything in common any more. Susan is a little surprised but inside she's glad that the situation is finally out in the open. After an hour of talking a lot of ground has been covered - for the first time in many years. The two of them finish their meal and Susan wonders how the evening will progress. Keith for his part switches on the TV, watches a program for half an hour and then goes to bed, without a word. Susan is almost histerical and shuts herself in the bathroom where she bursts into tears. Next morning Keith carries on as if nothing has happened between them. No word about yesterday, about the relationship. Susan feels even more misunderstood than before.

Perpetrator profile:

These individuals are emotionally cold and lack the skills necessary for a long-term partnership. Not surprisingly, they show little interest in the emotions of those around them. They ignore the other people who come into their lives. On the outside these ice-boxes are often highly respected, though this doesn't hide the fact that they are not good on the inter-personal level and tend to focus more on things than people.

They're only interested in their own well-being. They also have no access to their own emotional world and are excessively rational.

From a personality point of view one might say that such people are schizoid (not schizophrenic!), i.e., people who show little or no empathy, have no idea what the other person is trying to communicate, even when they cry or appeal to their emotions. They see the circumstances but not the feelings guiding them. All this prevents them from sharing the feelings of other people and makes it difficult for them to get in touch with their own emotional world. You can get down on your knees before them and see no reaction. These vampires are not intentionally cold but their victims suffer immensely.

Victim profile:

Victims fall into the emotional, people-oriented category, which means they're both sensitive and empathetic. They believe in good, appeal to others to be like-minded and can't understand why the other person doesn't understand them in return. They experience the vampire as an "emotional steamroller" or an "emotional iceberg".

The psychological mechanism:

Hyperrational versus emotional. Whenever the Ice-box Vampire appears people start to feel ignored and inferior. Ice-box Vampires captivate their audience with their inscrutability which gives them an air of mystery and ensures them a position of power. These people can't help the way they are but that doesn't exactly make the situation any easier. They often have no window to their emotional side and show the world a tough exterior. Sometimes the simple fact is that these people have different emotional needs. There are people who don't require much affection and attention at all – whatever the truth is, the more sensitive among us suffer as a result.

The problems described here often occur in one-to-one relationships – at the workplace and in a social context.

Antidote to Ice-box Vampires:

Try to restrain your feelings as much as possible when dealing with a rational person. Give up any hope of changing them, unless of course they want to change themselves. Meet rational people at the rational level, i.e. be objective, brief and clear. If you can, avoid revealing a lot about yourself and reduce contact to a minimum, or be prepared to suffer the consequences. Protect and develop your emotional nature by focussing on friendships with emotionally stable people! In the long term such relationships will be difficult to maintain – unless you change yourself and become the sort of person you would rather not be. In such marriages / partnerships it can prove very helpful if you try to satisfy your emotional needs (not your sexual ones please, that can lead to disaster) with a large circle of friends. This takes the strain off the partnership and in many cases allows it to survive (e.g. if there are small children and separation is not a good option).

The Ignorant Vampire

Some people talk to you without really talking to you. They aren't listening at all because they're basically not interested in you – although they pretend to for appearances' sake. We all know the situation: psychovampire asks you how you are. For a change you decide to give an honest answer and say something like: "Oh, not so bad. Not too well actually. I've felt better." Psychovampire replies: "Oh, I see, and what are you doing tomorrow? How's work?" You have walked straight into the trap and are now angry with yourself for being so open and honest.

A lot of talk about nothing: I

Bob meets an old friend Claire for a drink in his favourite bar. They haven't seen each other for quite a while. Claire's going through a difficult phase; she has trouble at work and has just recently terminated a 5-year relationship. It took her four attempts before she was finally able to cut the cord. While she feels relieved and proud of herself for making the break and ushering in a new phase in her life, she's weakened by a bout of flu and her energy levels are low. She sits in front of Bob sipping a gin and tonic she doesn't really want.

The situation:

Bob: "Hey, how are things with you then?"

Claire: "Oh, I don't normally complain but I haven't been feeling too well lately. I'm still recovering from the flu and I also finally took the plunge and separated from Klaus. It wasn't easy and I'm still getting over it, I guess."

Bob: "Hmm". He suddenly sees two other women enter the bar and welcomes them enthusiastically, "Hey, how are you? Long time, no see."

He invites them both to the table without asking Claire if it's okay with her and introduces everyone. He spends the next ten minutes talking to one of the two women. Though Claire doesn't feel much like small talk she's soon engaged in conversation with her neighbour.

Then Bob turns to Claire again and asks: "Are you OK?"

Claire looks into his apathetic eyes which betray quite different thoughts and just grants him a discreet nod. For her the evening is ruined. After only twenty minutes in the bar she feels drained and says goodbye to the group, frustrated and furious at the same time. She's heard nothing from Bob since.

A lot of talk about nothing: II

Mr. V. takes his wife to a party where they don't know 80 percent of the guests. A former colleague comes up to them and asks: "How are you?" The couple are unused to attending such occasions very often and are a little out of practice. It so happens that Mr. V.'s wife isn't feeling too good so she accepts the question at its face value and answers: "Not too bad". Her opposite isn't really listening and says: "I'm glad to hear it. Shall we go and join the others?"

Perpetrator profile:

These people overdo the multitasking and networking thing to such an extent that, when in groups, they can hardly concentrate on a topic. They're like a butterfly that flits to a new blossom every few seconds. On big occasions many people tend to fall into this kind of behaviour quite easily. Like all psychovampires, this vampire is not really interested in you as a person either, especially your innermost feelings and problems. The causes are varied: the psychovampire is only interested in his life and his concerns; or he doesn't want to hear anything about deeper rooted issues because then he would have to deal with them and - even worse for him – that would mean having to think about and reflect on his own inner self. His ability to relate to others is not so well developed – and that's being kind.

Victim profile:

Victims are sensitive people, well able to relate to others and not shy of opening up to others to express their feelings and engage in an intense exchange of ideas. But they are also the type of person who offers friendship and expects positive feedback in return in the form of encouragement, understanding and sympathy. After all, they would do the same.

The psychological mechanism:

The rather more superficial type comes up against the person with deeper feelings, or to put it another way, rational meets emotional. The Ignorant Psychovampire is generally occupied with his own self and not keen to get involved in deeper issues because he would then have to invest his precious time and energy. Contacts are only welcomed if they are in some way "valuable", like contact with a potential new customer. Such people are often underestimated – they might, for example, be professionally successful - and frequently overestimated. At work they have been known to disintegrate when, after an initial grand entrance, they're trusted to take on personnel responsibilities. Suddenly it's no longer enough to be result-oriented, they now have to cope with the needs, problems and mood variations of their co-workers.

In their private lives, this inability to relate at an emotional level is put to the test, for example, when the children grow up and material issues give way increasingly to more emotional ones. Suddenly it's not about feeding, clothing, etc., but about what the kids are going through at an emotional level – their feelings and anxieties - and getting involved in those can be quite a challenge!

Antidote for Ignorant Vampires:

Only open up when a situation is emotionally safe. Do not reveal everything immediately when you meet someone, put out a few feelers first. Don't always blame yourself. Some people are simply more rational than others.

The Himalaya Vampire

When good is never good enough for your father

Rebecca is a very successful investment banker, thirty something, married and recently mother to a son for whom she has given up her job. She's extremely discontented with her new role as "just a mum". Any self-esteem she has acquired up to now has been based on her achievements as a career woman in the outside world. In psychotherapy terms she understands that the reason for this thinking goes back to her childhood and to her relationship to her father in particular. She herself says on the subject: "I only really got my father's attention when I came home from school with good grades and kept out of mischief. Nobody in my family was interested if I had any friends or not. Each time I came home with good results he would want to know about the current class average. Only when my marks were much higher than the average did he occasionally praise me for my good performance. He wasn't in the least interested in my personal well-being as his daughter. When I turned 20 he once asked me if I was finally going to take my school leaving exams – I'd already taken them three years earlier - and passed. One of the things he used to say was: "Only the tough get to heaven." He would also say: "Tell me when you have your first 10,000 dollars in your account and then we'll talk again". I invested all my efforts to fulfil his wish and reached the sum by the time I was 30. It hasn't changed anything though. Even today, I still have the feeling that I have to earn the love of others. At home, I was never allowed to be lazy; I had to be constantly doing something productive."

When the boss drives his team to the summit

Donald P. is the boss of a PR agency and not known for praising his staff while demanding the impossible from them. He wants to involve them in his greatest ambition, to have the biggest PR agency in Berlin, but he doesn't notice that his team are not able and not willing to climb the summit with him. Donald had a similar childhood to Rebecca. In his father's eyes, his achievements were never good enough. Fluctuation in Donald's team of 40 people is around 25 percent – an exceptionally high rate. Personnel come and go fast when they realize that they can never do anything right for him. He himself rarely takes a holiday and then only a few days somewhere, but he never manages to relax: he reads his e-mails daily, makes calls on his cell phone while walking restlessly up and down the beach dictating new orders as the waves crash on the beach in the background. In reality, he's seldom satisfied with results despite his team working flat out to get the job done well. The best ones - and those are the people who refuse to be pushed into the role of victim – don't last long.

Perpetrator profile:

Achieving set targets is not enough for this high altitude vampire. He's only interested in performance and human achievement. This would be fine if only he didn't let others feel that performance and success are what really count in life and that happiness is unthinkable without them. "No pain, no gain" is one of his maxims. His expectations can never be satisfied, by anybody. He never allows himself a break and is permanently busy with the excuse that "there's always something that needs to be done." Such people are impossible to please, no matter how hard you try. Like Rebecca's father, Donald demands the impossible from himself too. He's in a constant state of activity, a sort of mania, and of course he expects the same input from others. People like Donald never relax inside. They rush from peak to peak and, paradoxically, never reach their goal (hence the name "Himalayas" because there is, so to speak, always a higher mountain to climb). Success is a short-lived experience because the next target is already lined up. People with this profile are often highly respected for their extremely competitive nature. Living together with them or having them as a colleague at work is very difficult and only functions well as long as you yourself continue to function. "I've had about ten girlfriends so far. We always get on great at the beginning, but after a while, about 3 or 4 months, they come to me with their problems; that's when I break off the relationship", the words of a 23-year-old student with anxiety disorders - and very competitive.

Victim profile:

This vampire's victims are very dependent on external influences and recognition by others. They're constantly striving to please their peers, give everything, and seldom get much back in return. Praise, recognition or regular salary increases are rare rewards, despite the flawless results they produce. They frequently succumb to the strong influence of the Himalayas Vampire, though they may not be aware of it, and the result is that they feel utterly drained. But instead of putting the blame on others they search their own souls for the mistakes, adding another nail to the coffin of their self-esteem. They are by nature very pleasant people but they pay for it with depleted energy reserves and low self-esteem.

The psychological mechanism:

As a rule, victims and perpetrators share the same emotional background. They experienced parental love as something conditional, in other words, it was not given unreservedly but was often coupled to achievement (good school grades) and/or good behaviour. This mechanism is described in greater detail in Chapter 5. Perpetrators have a very big influence throughout their victims' lives. Perpetrators and victims have an ambivalent respect for each other, holding each other in high regard for their respective achievements. However, when it comes to relationships they have little in common. I need to recognise that I deserve to be loved and do not have to constantly prove that it's good for me to be here and that I have a value which is not determined by what I achieve or how successful I am: if I can do that, I can free myself from the grasp of the Himalayas Vampire.

Antidote for Himalaya Vampires:

You will not change this vampire. Work on your self-esteem, if necessary seek therapeutic help. Make a firm resolution not to let others exercise so much power over you. Look for individuals who can be relied on to give you feedback and honest opinions, and who are important to you. Discuss important plans with these people and don't ask anyone else for their opinions.

At this point we'd like to introduce a technique which is particularly suitable for stress management in everyday life.

A side note: The Himalaya Phenomenon

At the top of the mountain you see two things: when you look back you see what you've achieved so far, when you look forward you see the next highest peak. Many will struggle back down again - often going right back down to the valley they started from - and then set off on the hard ascent of the next highest mountain. On reaching the summit they spy an even higher mountain and the process is repeated in a kind of vicious circle or - in psychodynamic terms - a neurotic repetition compulsion. The inability to find inner peace.

Putting this in career terms: there's always going to be a higher job to aim for; a striving for the highest possible position. There's always a bigger company, a more exciting project or a more ambitious plan – "once I have this job under my belt, I'll have more time for you and the children". In the language of financial security it is phrased like this: you can be even more secure with even more money. And in a partnership this comes out as: there's always a partner who looks better, is more successful, etc.

Possible interpretations:

To be certain of the kind of self-esteem and self-assurance which I gain from performing a service or from the appreciation of others for that service I'm willing to leap from summit to summit, perhaps without even wanting to. By employing this strategy I'm unconsciously trying to win more self-esteem and love. So I can't say no, I can't refuse others' requests for help, I take on every new challenge – after all, you can never have enough confidence and attention.

It also goes without saying that I can only "build a house" on a summit if I consciously resolve to stay there - for a certain period of time at least. I can only build up a deep relationship with a partner if I make a conscious decision to do so - even though there may be a number of 'better alternatives'- and I am willing to commit myself completely. As long as I keep changing from one partner to the next – true to the maxim: "Things will be better with the next one" - I will never find a deeper (and fulfilling) relationship.

For me it is vital that, although I feel the urge to go on and climb the next summit, I consciously decide not to - even when faced with strong opposition from family and friends: "You can't refuse promotion!"

The Polite Vampire

Brandon began his new job at a PR company in January. The first few months were phenomenal from his point of view. His team was open for ideas which meant he was able to implement them on his own initiative. He got positive feedback from his boss C. Meyer. His gut feeling told him: I can stay here longer than in the other jobs. But it wasn't to be so.

Brandon's CV had been anything but predictable in recent times. He changed jobs every two years, in some cases after six months. His moves were not voluntary, his bosses gave him notice. The official reason was: unsatisfactory time management. The real, hidden reasons: frequent stress symptoms and subsequent absences through illness. Weighed down by this bundle of chain reactions, Brandon frequently failed to deliver his work on time - an unacceptable shortcoming in the eyes of his superiors.

It was the same story in his latest job; Brandon couldn't meet the demands of his boss. He was repeatedly called away to deal with new problems at home which only he was able to take care of, in his view at least. This led him to be absent several afternoons a week. On one occasion there was no hot water in the house. Brandon doesn't live alone. He's happily married and has a son. Money wasn't an issue. And yet, he seemed to attract disaster. Or did the real truth lie elsewhere? Was he perhaps just a little clumsy when it came to solving problems? Everyone's hot water system – a vampire's too – can break down once in a while. But for a certain kind of psychovampire finding a solution to problems always seems to be a more complicated and costlier business than for others. What we have here is the Polite Psychovampire, the type of person who would normally never be taken for a vampire because they're so friendly and obliging - too obliging. They want to please everybody and get bogged down in acts of kindness, driven by nothing more than the inner urge to be extraordinarily obliging. One spin-off of this is that they become enormous time-wasters. The Polite Vampire is considerate and self-sacrificing. In his references this quality would be described with the words: "Was always there when you needed him and always did his best." No word about finding a quick and effective solution to a problem.

These vampires are clearly hiding a deficit, something they also manage to do with great success. What the actual shortcoming is soon becomes apparent – sometimes sooner, sometimes it takes a while. In the case of Brandon's boss, Meyer, the time span was relatively short because he, fatally, turned out to be the direct opposite of Brandon - a quick, focused Himalayas Vampire - with fatal results. If Meyer's hot water had packed up he would not have sacrificed one single afternoon for it - he would have delegated the problem, taking into account the - in his view - secondary risk of coming across as the impolite and arrogant type who lets others do his work for him.

How the safety hook of a Himalayas Vampire can ultimately snap is demonstrated in the next episode of the employer-employee Brandon-Meyer relationship: the cause of many of Brandon's frequent absences from work was his son who in Meyer's opinion was pampered by his father. He would go into detailed descriptions of why he had to be away from the office: "Yesterday I had to go to the child psychologist with my 6-year-old son because he was a victim of sexual harassment by a girl two years older than him. She pushed him into a small room without a light and touched him indecently. The child psychologist ruled that the girl's assaults had to be stopped in order to protect other younger pupils at school. If not her attacks could spread to the whole class...". (In the interests of our readers we will omit the rest of the story.) Had Meyer not stopped him with: "Well, it's quite normal and acceptable at that age for minors to discover their bodies and each other", he would have carried on talking all afternoon. How did he hear about it, asked Meyer out of interest. His son had told the family everything in detail. Meyer was disinclined to classify this story as a dramatic or traumatic experience, especially when the child had obviously not felt the urge to conceal something avoidable and disagreeable. In Meyer's way of thinking children do not speak voluntarily and in detail about disagreeable events.

The more drastic outcome for him and his team was that Brandon deemed it absolutely necessary to take his son out of school for three days and look after him personally at home. In short, he stayed away from the office and left a whole heap of work on his project undone and it was already way behind schedule. The really unacceptable aspect of all this for Meyer, and the situation as a whole, was that he saw no real reason for Brandon's absenteeism, did not therefore respect his behaviour and lost patience with Brandon again – to say nothing of his dwindling respect for him. One consequence of this was that he dreamt of Brandon one night. He was standing in front him and shouting at him as loud as he could (or so it seemed to him when he woke) using words to shake some sense into him. He as a Himalayas Vampire had bottled up so much fury inside that he had now reached bursting point, at least subconsciously in his sleep – he could just as easily have climbed up Mount Everest in one night.

Perpetrator profile and Victim profile:

In this unique combination both vampire types become perpetrator and victim at the same time. For the Himalayas Psychovampire nothing can happen fast enough (see previous chapter). The summit chaser values unrelenting diligence, which has its price. In this case the price is a lack of understanding and, ultimately, tolerance for the personal life of the 'polite' colleague who tries to appease everyone and, in the particular instance of the Himalayas Vampire, is destined to fail miserably.

In stark contrast, the Polite Vampire drives the Himalayas Vampire to the edge of insanity with his, in Meyer's eyes, incredibly time-consuming escapades solving (or not solving) private problems - especially when this takes an inordinately long time - and which add further strength to the main shortcoming of the Himalayas Vampire, which is his lack of tolerance for the slower course of action.

The psychological mechanism:

The Polite Vampire is blessed with a personality structure that can often best be described as conformist, self-conscious and avoidant. Early on in life he had to learn to adapt, put others' needs before his own, be there for others, make them happy and not take centre stage. This often happens in families where parental love and affection was a conditional experience. But it also applies to families in which you were not permitted to make mistakes because the consequences were either punishment or denial of affection. These victims had to learn to function well and not draw attention to themselves; they were never allowed to express their own needs. They had to give way to others and their opinion never counted. Over the course of years this naturally led to insecurity, low self-esteem, inability to make decisions and the feeling of always having to have a safety net. Such people are very friendly and a pleasure to be with, on the one hand. The downside is that they are quickly overstretched. In the long run, their constant need to please everyone releases aggression in their peers.

Antidote for the Polite Vampire:

Never criticize the Polite Vampire because this will start a vicious circle and he will try to make even greater efforts to conform even more in order to make himself popular with you. What's more, don't ask him too often what he'd do in a certain situation. That puts too many demands on him, which in turn increases his insecurity and releases feelings of angst. Make decisions for him, give him instructions but do so in such a way that he has the chance to express his own opinion.

If you want to help the Polite Vampire with lasting effect you must create an emotionally safe atmosphere in which he feels so confident in your presence that he can express any (self-) doubts and voice any needs.

This is a long process - not quite unlike a course of therapy - but a very effective one. The only thing is that hardly anyone at work is likely to go to such trouble.

The Expert Vampire

This expert is no expert although he's convinced he knows the answers to many of life's questions. Here are three family stories all based on true occurrences.

The Ignorant Expert

Ryan works on big projects for an international concern. Over the years his job has led him to become something of a cosmopolitan. Now, however, the financing for his current project is in danger. At a big family celebration on the occasion of his parents' golden wedding his brother-in-law Alexander, who has a quiet job in a government office, is also present. Alexander asks him how things are going and Ryan tells him briefly about the scale of the project. In his enthusiasm he fails at first to notice that Alexander isn't listening to him at all; he asks no questions, turns his gaze away to look around the room at other members of the family and, to be honest, is bored. His only comment: "Yes, we have all stress. Even at work there's a lot of stress. Our local government office is due to merge with another district and nobody knows what will happen. And now we have to work 40 hours a week instead of the present 38.5 hours, and we don't get a 14th month's salary anymore either." The fact that Ryan works 70 hours a week, that his job is endangered, that he only receives a low basic salary and the rest is dependent on performance and hard figures, is something he finds difficult to bring home to his brother-in-law. This exchange, which really wasn't one, leaves Ryan feeling totally drained.

The expert with universal tips

Alexander's brother, Boris, is his own boss and has built up a small business with 40 employees. In recent months Boris has had to dismiss some long-standing employees after the demands made on the workforce by new developments had risen steeply and the employees wouldn't agree to help implement changes and actively support them. Now he's going through the motions of taking on new staff who have the qualifications for the job. At the same family gathering he tells everyone about this new start. His cousin Jeff, who works in a bank, makes a comment along the lines that Boris should have done things differently: "You can't just get rid of these people after so many years," he says amazed. "Did they steal the golden spoons, or what? In a family enterprise like yours you just can't go around dismissing people like that. What do the other workers say?"

Perpetrator profile:

These kind of people think that their world and their opinions are transferable to others. In doing so they present themselves as experts on other people's affairs. Typically, they are very rational and egocentric with low self-esteem and find it nigh on impossible are put themselves in a situation that someone else is going through. There are also Expert Vampires who look on others with envy because they have achieved more, because they took more risks. They themselves tend to be more careful and anxious and this gives them the need to criticize their contemporaries. After all, if this psychovampire type were to admit that the other person was really in a worse off position than himself, he would have to admit to himself at the same time that his problems were not so great. This would have fatal consequences: he would probably have to change his life or the negative attitude he had until then.

Victim profile:

Whoever allows himself to be drained by this vampire often suffers from self-doubt because, in reality, it's clear that the world as experienced by one person is different from the one experienced by another. This means that such statements should, theoretically, not be taken too seriously. The person who finds himself in an emotionally weakened position, like Boris or Ryan, is open to doubt – even when this comes from outside. Expert Vampires have a particularly great influence on us in stress situations because they sense our own doubts - and use this information to unsettle us. The victim has a latent bad conscience even before the conversation begins and this is strengthened by the psychovampire's statements, however unqualified they may be.

The psychological mechanism:

The Expert Psychovampire increases any doubts the victim has about his own actions and drags him even further down. He only has this power though because we give it to him. We give him the status of expert and allow him to influence us with his opinions. People of a sensitive and reflective nature are particularly susceptible to the Expert Vampire.

The au pair and the grandmother

Rachel went to spend a year in the South of France as an au pair and really struck gold with her guest family. She got on very well with the two children and the parents. At mealtimes they would laugh a lot and soon built up a good trusting relationship. One member of the family was different though and didn't quite fit in with the harmonious group: the grandmother of the two children - on the mother's side. She was a small, lively, busy woman who knew everything better than her daughter, her son-in-law, her grandchildren - and the au pair. She was consistently telling her 38-year-old daughter Eliane what to do despite the fact that as doctor and mother of two children she was firmly in control of her life.

One Saturday morning Rachel had been given the honor of preparing the family dinner for the whole week-end. This included making a flan, a dessert, which was to be the cause of a small drama that was to unfold in the kitchen when Grandma appeared unexpectedly on the scene and proceeded to inspect the contents of the saucepans. Before long she discovered what she called a disaster as she watched Rachel prepare the flan. Without being asked, she gave Rachel tips on how to make the dish. Rachel began to boil inside and suddenly thrust the wooden spoon into grandmother's hand and left the house in silent anger.

Rachel never saw the grandmother again for the rest of her stay in the house. She was lucky not to be a member of the family for when she dropped by on a surprise visit three years later during a vacation with her own family, she found the house empty of children. Eliane wasn't there either. Instead, the father was sitting there alone and when she asked him what had happened he told her in one short, sad sentence: "Eliane strangled her own mother in a fit of anger".

Perpetrator profile:

This exceedingly dramatic and sad – but unfortunately true example – shows the destructive effect extreme Expert Psychovampires can have, particularly on those close to them.

Victim profile:

The reactions of the two victims, Rachel and Eliane, were very different. While Rachel, more or less as an outsider, could easily dissociate herself from the vampire and, moreover, as au pair led a much more relaxed life than Eliane, the latter found it extremely difficult to distance herself from her own mother – in reality it was virtually impossible. Many sons and daughters do however succeed in severing relations with their parents. Our society tends to view broken families as a disgrace. The question begging itself here though is whether a bitter end like this one is not, ultimately, the real disgrace.

The psychological mechanism:

For people with strong emotional ties who are under severe pressure, an Expert Vampire can be the trigger which drives them insane, in the truest sense of the word.

Antidote to the Expert Vampire:

Analyze the criticism of these "experts" to see if they are in fact adequately qualified. Before I give somebody the right to take the stage as an expert, I first need to be convinced that he is an expert and that I have asked for his advice. It's far better to choose someone in your life whose judgment you can really count on.

Dance of the Vampires: a management team made up of Nosey Vampire, Wolf-In-Sheep's-Clothing Vampire and It-Wasn't-Me Vampire.

Imagine for a moment that there are three employees in a company; one is always sticking his nose into other people's business although this is totally unnecessary and amazingly time-consuming; the second is the boss but he's incapable of accepting responsibility for his actions and has perfected the art of never being guilty of mistakes while appearing to play a considerable role in the company's successes; and the third is just plain hypocritical. Would you want to share your workplace with these people? If you're honest, you wouldn't. But what happens if you start a job and a few months after completing your trial period find yourself faced with a situation you are uncomfortable with? Here's the story of an observer (a secretary) employed in a company supplying parts to the automobile industry.

In company X an important customer puts in a complaint about a wrong delivery of car parts. As (bad) luck would have it, the parts he mistakenly received were initially intended for his biggest competitor. Michael, the boss of the small company, is exasperated: "This is really embarrassing, guys; it should never have happened", he rages in front of Sheila and Nigel. Both exchange unsure looks and ask who was responsible for the contract with the customer. Michael, getting very worked up, rolls his eyes and replies that he's not the only one who signs the contracts, Nigel does too, as everybody knows. Nigel, the Nosey Vampire, may have the personality of a private detective and always knows what's going on but in this particular instance he really didn't know a lot about the contract. Michael, aware of Nigel's excessive interest in everything that happens around him, now accuses him of negligence: "At management level we are all responsible. This means that everybody has to be on the ball, all the time." For a moment there's silence. "And who signed the contract then?", asks Sheila, courageously trying to bring some clarity to the matter. Michael gets even angrier and is forced to admit that - due to holiday absences - he completed the transaction alone. The astonishing thing about this for Sheila and Nigel is that Michael succeeds in giving them both the feeling that they are just as guilty for the embarrassing incident: three times he repeats that in middle management everyone is duty bound to take full responsibility at all times. His almost biblical repetition of this annoys Nigel who defends himself: "We would if we had the time", he remarks, forgetting for a moment that he's the one constantly poking his nose into matters which have little to do with his duties at Quality Control. Nigel is ultimately saved by the fact that he was on vacation in the South of France where luckily he was sticking his nose into bottles of red wine and perfume on the day the products left the company premises.

Michael on the other hand is never one to surrender when it comes to covering up his own mistakes and defending his honour, so at the same meeting he finds a new reason for shifting his guilt to others. He digs up a case going back three months which is of relatively minor importance in comparison to the mistaken delivery. That time it was the fault of a recently appointed temp, a student, who for once forgot to switch on the company answering machine - the day before a local public holiday. This act of omission would not have taken a dramatic turn had Nigel not chosen this day to go to work and found himself having to do telephone duty for half a day. This had got him so worked up that he went to Michael to complain. True to his character, Michael's first reaction was defensive and he furiously denied any responsibility for the fact that the temp hadn't been correctly familiarized with her duties, although this was normally his job. He blamed Nigel instead. The fact that Nigel couldn't have known that the temp hadn't been shown the ropes should really have confirmed Nigel's doubts about his boss's managerial skills – but Michael was far from admitting any such thing. As an It-Wasn't-Me Vampire he was unable, on principle, to take responsibility for mistakes.

Nigel, for his part, attracted attention in the firm as an all-knowing, ever-present and prying individual; as a Nosey Vampire he was, in fact, digging his own "grave". He was busy digging it for others too. He simply could not resist enquiring about the reasons for a colleague's absence and then checking to see if it was true. His job in Quality Control didn't seem to overstretch his abilities, with the result that he just had to keep tabs on everyone and everything. And so he created a culture of mistrust which in the end proved counter-productive because the colleagues in whose presence he was so interested were not connected to his particular job and many suspected that he was checking on them by order of the boss, and consequently they avoided Nigel, purely for reasons of self-protection.

But neither his work in Quality Control nor his "surveillance work" were enough to sate Nigel's thirst for knowledge. He regularly interfered in discussions which had nothing to do with him. He also played colleagues off against each other by making remarks which were then interpreted as (un-)official information. It gave him considerable pleasure to unnerve other people with his smooth talking and misinformation.

Sheila didn't fall for Nigel's games; she was immune to the Nosey Vampire because as a Wolf-In-Sheep's-Clothing Vampire she had her own crusade to follow. If what she used was really a weapon or simply her true nature, is irrelevant here. Her game was even more subversive. She went around with a permanent smile on her face and never failed to ask how you were, in an excessively friendly manner. As soon as she noticed that her own interests were in danger and an open conflict was about to erupt, her smiles were replaced by an expression that was almost evil. With this wolf's face she was suddenly a different person. Whenever a customer put in a complaint, she refused to accept any responsibility either.

What made her actions worse was the way she stalked colleagues in Customer Service with her over friendly and butter-wouldn't-melt-in-her-mouth sheep's face, asking them seemingly innocent questions and then emerging from her sheep's coat and unfairly calling these colleagues to account for their actions. That she was in the wrong was clear from the fact that she had no interest in the truth at all. She was happy to accept the opinion of the infuriated customer and wasn't interested with hearing her colleague's version of the story. The customer is king so he gets a full hearing and is always right. Her reputation among the workers suffered as a result; they avoided her in droves because they couldn't bear the pressure or her falseness any longer. For years Sheila had to struggle with the problem of colleagues deserting her team, particularly the good ones.

Michael's constant urge to shift responsibility to others led him one day to sell Sheila the "prestigious and important office" of deputy manager. The problem was that he failed to inform the whole team that he now had a deputy. Sheila proudly accepted her new role while continuing to spy on her colleagues. She duly lost even more sympathy points when it finally came out that she was acting on the orders of her boss. In the end the pressure became too much for her and she left the company after a relatively short time in office.

All the people who remained faithful to Michael's company over the years underwent gradual changes. The question which presents itself is: did he turn them all into vampires? Did he force them without their full knowledge and volition to adopt vampire-like survival tactics?

Perpetrator and victim profiles:

The Nosey Vampire

This type sticks his nose into all sorts of things that are really the concern of other people – and certainly not his. His compulsion to interfere, however unnecessarily, in the lives of others leads - if for the most part unintentionally - to chaos and countless misunderstandings among the many, senselessly involved victims he drags into his rather insignificant stories. To feed his own low self-esteem he craves to be informed about everything and everybody. Nosey Vampires occur in families too. If you want to spread some gossip he's the right address. With his own personal "news agency" he can broadcast the news straightaway, even though it may just be tainted by his interpretation of events. His victims are quickly on to him and try to limit the information they pass on to, or withhold from, him - but their efforts are generally in vain.

Antidote for nasal vampires:

Once you have identified somebody as "a news agency" be extremely careful about the news you pass on. We can learn a thing or two from politicians and diplomats here: "No comment". This is the best and most effective way to cut out the Nosey Vampire. After all, what is even the best news agency without news?

The other real danger is that you could become a psychovampire yourself and find yourself forming an alliance with the Nosey Vampire. Be on your guard.

The Wolf In Sheep's Clothing Vampire

This one is deceitful but outwardly always friendly, so he's misjudged by many. While some people are underestimated, this contemporary is often overestimated. How can you recognise him? The only way is to pay close attention to your own sense of perception, your gut feeling. Unfortunately, our inner voice can also be completely wrong. This makes feedback from others very important. If your opposite number is being honest with you, his perception can help us to objectify our own perception. It's also worth paying attention to the reaction a person releases in you, what effect they have on you, how you feel in their company, or how you feel when that person is not present any more. If negative feelings come to the surface, be careful.

Antidote for the Wolf-In-Sheep's-Clothing Vampire:

As so often in life, the best strategy for survival here is: keep a healthy distance. Don't let yourself be taken in again and again by this kind of person, especially when their excellent camouflage makes them hard to expose. And even when others praise them to the hilt because they show concern and seem to have a great sense of responsibility: for you this person is a psychovampire.

The It-Wasn't-Me Vampire

These vampires are very strenuous for those around them because they don't look for solutions; instead they repeatedly protest that they are not the cause of mistakes. Why would someone go to such pains to convince everyone else that they're not responsible? Such people always look for a culprit and won't rest until they've found one. They themselves always have a clear conscience.

Unfortunately, these people are none too skilled in the art of inner reflection, or shall we say that this ability is not yet fully developed, and so they are able to block out a thought that could in any way be a reflection on themselves and their behaviour patterns. This is very exhausting for their social counterparts. With all the evidence lying, as it were, spread out on the table everybody knows exactly who the "perpetrator" is. Some of these energy suckers even have the ability to change unnoticed from perpetrator to victim, with the result that their opposite is suddenly the one who feels guilty. We frequently observe this in relationships. After living in conflict with your partner for a number of years, you begin to ask yourself if maybe there's something wrong with you. This can be true of course; it's also just as likely, however, that you've been living all these years with an It-Wasn't-Me Vampire.

Antidote for the It-Wasn't-Me Vampire:

Accept that this person is the way he is. That sounds a bit simple and it is (putting it into practise is all the more challenging). This psychovampire will continue to be true to character for the rest of his life - and will succeed too. Any attempts at conversion are doomed to failure.

PART 2

CHAPTER 4

Vampire Exposure

Why do you wonder that globe-trotting does not help you,
seeing that you always take yourself with you?

(Socrates)

The case studies in the preceding chapter provide an overview of the mechanisms and variations of vampirism and the victim's behaviour patterns. They also reveal situations in which psychovampirism is likely to occur. In the particular example of Eliane, who kills her mother, we can see how dangerous psychovampirism can be when it remains undetected and occurs repeatedly in our immediate environment, and what happens if no attention is paid to the psychovampires and everything is suppressed. Most people, victims or psychovampires, are not aware of this mechanism at all, which means that exposing the psychovampire is already half way to rendering him harmless. The psychovampire operates, so to speak, as if he were wearing a magic hood whereby the trick is to remove this hood and, even if you do not expose him publicly as a psychovampire, then do so at least for yourself and treat him differently from that moment on.

How often do we hear someone say of an exhausting acquaintance: "My God, doesn't Ms. P. or Mr. P. wear you down?" We're not sensitized enough to reflect more deeply on this outburst and this is dangerous because the psychovampire functions like a leak in a gasoline tank: you can drive a long way but you'll have to constantly refuel because consumption has risen. The same applies to life energy; it takes a few years or decades before you're surprised to find that you've become chronically exhausted, drained, tired and perhaps even depressive. The perception that someone comes across as exhausting is - like all perceptions – a purely subjective evaluation which is not applicable to everyone. In other words: the psychovampires featured in the preceding case studies are not universally identified perpetrators. Let us recall: Bob may be an Ignorant Psychovampire to some, to others he seems attentive and "normal". And Bob can suddenly become the victim of an Expert Vampire while others are immune to this vampire type and do not perceive him in the same way. In relationships one can observe this phenomenon all too well: one partner is experienced as very exhausting and this can lead to interminable quarrels, but after a separation this same partner gets on like a house on fire with the new partner.

Short, repeated attacks leave permanent marks

One warning signal is valid for all vampire types: in an apparently innocent situation - a brief encounter or a short incident - a lot of our energy is disproportionately sucked away. Since it happens within a short time span we tend to quickly forget this short-lived experience. And there's the rub! We must learn to pick up and quantify these moments with full awareness. In Positive Psychotherapy we speak of so-called micro-traumas, i.e. little things to which we at first attach no meaning but which build up into something that ultimately affects us in a negative way, along the lines of: 'little strokes fell big oaks'. We can all resist a single attack from a psychovampire but when you have to face them on a daily basis and over several years, they will eventually take their toll.

There are many examples which illustrate the unique instances when a vampire bites home and which, if they occur repeatedly, cause lasting damage; here are some:

Mr. Weasel is 47 years old and owns a medium-sized company in the service industry. He has a workforce of 50, travels a lot, attends plenty of meetings and works 10-12 hours a day. He's a happy-go-lucky soul, invariably in a good mood, copes reasonably well with job-related stress, does a lot of sport and is in a pretty good condition. Mr. Weasel's report:

"When I come home after a working day I'm pretty tired but not exhausted. I'm glad to see my family, to spend some time with the children and then talk about the day with my wife. The trouble is that I'm hardly home before I notice my energy levels starting to drop - after only a few minutes. My wife's a really nice person but she often feels overworked, screams at the children, complains a lot and is always stressed out. The house is usually in a mess and she gets appointments mixed up. As soon as I get home she hands responsibility for the kids over to me and takes it easy for the rest of the evening. This leaves me to organise not only the children but also to defuse the moment and restore a positive atmosphere – and my mind is still at the office. As if this wasn't enough my wife shouts at me a lot, telling me I can't do anything right and constantly reproaching me for leaving her to do all the household chores. The first 5 minutes at home cost me more energy than my whole 10-hour working day.

Last week my wife spent the day at her parents'. You won't believe this but the situation was much more relaxed; the children were in a great mood, we played for a while before I took them to bed and then did some reading and watched TV and ended the day completely relaxed. What shall I do? I'd really prefer to get a divorce but with the children this is probably not a good option."

Time plays no role in this bloodsucker story.
It's the intensity of the situation, i.e.
a one-minute encounter with a
psychovampire that can use up the
equivalent of a whole day's
energy. Whenever a meeting or
situation consumes a disproportionate
amount of energy you could be right in
thinking that a psychovampire has just struck.

Warning signs for the "wordless" vampire

When you get home in the evening feeling exhausted and you don't know why you're so tuckered although it was quite a normal day, the chances are that you have crossed paths with a psychovampire. And if your mood, which was good until then, suddenly and without recognizable cause takes a dip, it may be that a psychovampire has tapped into your energy at some point without you noticing it. It doesn't always need a verbal exchange for you to feel the bite. Sometimes just thinking of a certain person or the mention of a name makes us feel faint as the energy drains away. If you have a whole bunch of appointments and meetings for work one after the other on the same day merely looking at the list in the morning and suddenly reading the name "xy" at 5th place on your list can cause you to utter the words "Oh my God. Not him again". The chances are then ten to one that you're dealing with a psychovampire.

The following case illustrates the effect of the 'wordless' psychovampire:

Dominique D. (34, marketing assistant) is making an important presentation. She spent days preparing for it. The presentation is going well. After half an hour her boss enters the room, gives her a sign to continue (meaning: "Don't let me put you off. I'm not here at all") and sits down at the back of the room. Dominique D. continues but her confidence has left her and so has her humor. The pleasant atmosphere which pervaded the room up to now suddenly evaporates and Dominique D's words don't flow as easily any more. All her energy seems to have vanished as she becomes conscious of the need to choose her words very carefully in the presence of her boss. He's known to be resentful and capable of the occasional fit or unexpected outburst of anger. Within a short time of his stepping into the room Dominique feels utterly drained. A psychovampire has struck, although he hasn't uttered a single word. In all likelihood her boss isn't even aware of his psychovampiric effect.

The Universal Vampire

In most cases - roughly 90 percent – psychovampirism is a very personal encounter; I alone experience a person as a vampire, others might too, or maybe not at all. So you might get a situation where friend A says to friend B: "I don't know what's wrong with you. Kyle is a really nice guy, he always brings you flowers, is so polite and friendly when he meets you. I can't understand why you want to break things off. Maybe it's something to do with you; you have a problem with men. Kyle is not only nice, he looks good too". From being the perpetrator (in the eyes of the woman who's leaving him), he now suddenly becomes a victim (the woman leaves him which makes him outwardly appear as the victim). Outsiders often fail to comprehend why I experience somebody as exhausting because the experience is subjective and closely connected to my biography and my own special personality structure.

Yet, when it comes to the universal vampire, subjective perception is the same for everybody, or is at least universally similar. Everybody experiences him as a strain on the nerves and this universality takes away some of his power. The magic hood has been removed, so to speak, and he's treated as a kind of eccentric, not as a threat.

Here's the example of a situation with a universal vampire:

Christmas is on the doorstep and the whole family wants to celebrate together. Everyone is actually looking forward to seeing all four families at their grandparents' home on the same day. Grandfather (78) is an affable, easily "manageable" type and always good for a surprise, while grandma (75) can sometimes be a strain on the nerves. As a perfectionist she demands a lot from herself and others, placing a lot of value on punctuality and order and reacting in a gruff manner when something doesn't suit her. All the members of the family know this and try to be punctual. The grandchildren have been instructed not to throw their things around or leave them lying anywhere; nobody wants "to upset Grandma". You could liken granny to a universal vampire; if, for example, somebody won a trip for two, she'd probably be the last to be invited whereas everyone would want to take grandpa. But because all the family members know that granny is "difficult" and fully comply to her wishes and don't expect her to change overnight, her influence and power over the others is much reduced, even though she doesn't know this. Nevertheless, she is and will remain a handful to all concerned.

Typical vampire talk

Essentially, people communicate on two levels: the objective level (objective-rational level) and the relationship level (emotional level). The psychovampire always strikes at the relationship level, in 100% of the cases. At the objective level it's possible to have completely different opinions but once it becomes personal, insults, disappointments, aggressions and other feelings rise to the surface.

Here are some of the typical psychovampire statements you should be familiar with in order to identify potential vampires fast:

- "I'd never have thought that of you."
- "I thought you were a true friend."
- "You're my last hope. If you don't help me, no one else will".
- "You always have time for your employees and your customers but you never have time for me and the kids."
- "When your secretary has a small problem you spend hours solving it with her."
- "When I was new in the company I was like you too, I had loads of ideas."
- "We've always done it this way."
- "Wait until you have as much experience as I have, then you'll understand."
- "Today's youth, full of go but no experience."
- "You've always got time for your patients."
- "I'm disappointed in you. You're no different / better than the rest."
- "Perhaps you should ask yourself if you're in the right place / if this is the right job for you.
- "I thought we were friends."
- "You're just like the others and I thought you were different."
- "Things were better in the old days."

- "Somebody came up with that idea years ago."
- "I helped you when you needed it, is it too much to expect the same in return?"
- "It's OK if you don't have time for my problems. You've got a lot on your plate at the moment and it's much more important than my affairs."
- "I'm sorry for bothering you with my problems. There are others who need your help more urgently."
- "Don't worry if you don't have time for me. It wasn't so important."

Be on your guard: all these statements could also come from a "non-vampire" and are meant honestly and sincerely - though they often contain a hint of vampirism too.

Identification stages

The first step to take if you want to expose a psychovampire is to analyze your own social environment and your day to day challenges. Evaluate your everyday life / daily routine and establish what, who and which situations drain your energy.

Vampiric people

The next step is to recognize the vampires in special environment. You can be surrounded by a psychovampire for 30 years without being fully aware of it, which means you could be letting yourself be sucked dry over and over again:

1) Try to identify the people around you, do it spontaneously and make a note of the people you "suspect" of being a vampire to you. Which people in your direct surroundings are, if you're honest, exhausting? Whose contact would you like to reduce or even avoid? Be frank and truthful with yourself, it may involve people close to you like husband, parents, children, boss, etc., in other words, people you can't blot out of your life so easily,

who you are morally obliged to love and respect and can never openly call a vampire. Write down the names of those people whose very name causes negative feelings like, "Oh God, not him again," or makes you say, "Tell him I'm not here," or to take action, "Quick, let's go out the back way, before she arrives".

2) Note down the names of those with whom you have close contact and who other people find exhausting but who in your eyes are – for whatever reason – not psychovampires.

3) List the names of those with whom you come in daily contact and don't miss when they're occasionally absent.

4) Write down the names of those without whom the meeting (consultation, conference or discussion) runs more smoothly, positively and more quickly than when they are present.

Vampiric situations

Certain situations can be energy sucking in themselves. Which recurring situations do you experience as "stressful"?

To illustrate this here's a personal experience from Russia:

"When one of the authors (H.P.) travelled through the USSR for six months at the beginning of the 1990s to hold lectures and seminars at different universities, conditions were far from favorable. As he relates: "There was little to eat, I couldn't speak a word of Russian, hardly anybody spoke English, I was in a different city every week, it was cold, as low as minus 20 degrees at times, communication with the outside world was virtually impossible (no cell phones, no e-mail, a catastrophic telephone system) - to name but a few drawbacks. After the first 6-month trip – it later became eight years - I carried out an 'energy evaluation' for myself. To my complete surprise I found that it wasn't the cold, the hunger, the linguistic obstacles or the loneliness that drained away so much of my energy; the real culprit was the accommodation. At that time hotels hardly existed so during my travels I spent each night in the home of my Russian hosts. This gave me a first-hand opportunity to experience, and appreciate, Russian hospitality. But the apartments were very small, with just two rooms, which generally meant that I spent the nights in the living room – usually a connecting room. Everybody had to go through this room to get to the kitchen or the bathroom - people and pets alike. After a day of long seminars I needed some rest and a place to "chill out" but I didn't find it there. Evenings were spent in the close family circle talking intensively about marital problems, mental problems, etc. which the hosts were keen to discuss with me. At first, politeness dictated that I accepted the offer of a bed which meant putting myself in a stressful situation. After I'd taken stock of my position in the spring of 1992 it became clear that the overnight ritual had perhaps robbed me of more than 70 percent of my energy - and this led me to change my approach from summer 1992. I wrote to the organizers of forthcoming seminars and stated - to their great astonishment - that I'd like to spend the night at a hotel or their version of a hall of residence. They were reluctant to agree to my wish, partly because student hostels were very basic - often without water, little or no heating and dangerous. But for me it was a liberating moment. In the evening, after being dropped off I could enter the room, close (lock!) the door and spread out - emotionally and physically. In spite of the cold (the hostels were seldom warmer than about 60°) it was wonderful - and life-energy saving."

Other examples of "vampire" situations could be the daily traffic jam on the way to work, problems at home or the mess on your desk.

Three methods can expose them: Are you a victim?

The following suggestions will offer some insight as you reflect on the possibility that you're being plagued by psychovampires.

1st Method:

Draw up a list of your regular activities dividing it in 3 columns: time / energy / money, and ask yourself systematically:

- How much time do I need for a certain job / activity / project?
- How much energy, strength, thought etc. must I invest in this job, or how much energy does the job take from me?
- What are the financial benefits? (There are many people who invest a lot of time in countless acts of voluntary work and have no time to do the really important things.)

Should you, for example, be investing a lot of energy in one activity and have little time for others, it could mean that a psychovampire is hovering somewhere in your immediate vicinity. Should you be using small amounts of energy but still have little time for other things, it may mean that a vampire is also gnawing away at you unnoticed. Naturally there are certain areas of life which require a lot of energy but as a counter-balance there must be areas that are real energy boosters.

2ⁿᵈ Method:

Identify the difference between important and urgent duties which occupy you daily. Observe your activities during one week and create a list with the following scale:

- important and urgent
- not important and urgent
- not important and not urgent
- important and not urgent

This is a well-established practice from the world of time management. Experience shows that we spend about half our time on matters which are not important to us but often vital to others. If 60% of your answers come under "not important and urgent" you're obviously spending your time doing favors for others. You can't say no and you let your life be ruled by those around you. Don't forget that efficient and self-determined behaviour distinguishes itself in the execution of important matters! A psychovampire could by trying to attack you at the emotional level, exploit your bad conscience or eat away at your self-esteem ("Can you do this for me, please. I have no one else to turn to. No one can do it as well as you. If you don't help me, I don't know what I'll do.").

3rd Method:

You could be surrounded by a psychovampire if the following situations apply:

- You sense that other people have too big an influence on you, on your well-being, on your self-esteem or on your behaviour. If you react with unusual intensity to a (minor) situation, this could also be a sign. Example: Somebody makes a remark like "typical woman" and you're offended, you can't stop thinking about it and you let it disturb your concentration.
- Your mood on that day was fairly stable but one short encounter with somebody is sufficient to disperse this positive frame of mind. Once again: make a daily list with the names of these people and the situations in which you encounter them.
- You find yourself getting into the same situation with the same person over and over again and every time you feel bad afterwards because the same little game has been played and you're angry with yourself. (As in the example in Chapter 1, Situation 3: A student comes home for the week-end. She wants to tell her parents all about the university and the experiences she's been having and has hardly begun when her parents interrupt her and ask if she's getting enough to eat, what the weather's like, etc. This pattern repeats itself every time and the student feels misunderstood.)
- You notice that whenever you're together with a certain person a sort of remote control takes over your behaviour. Ask yourself in whose presence you suddenly feel that your have surrendered control although you are, generally speaking, a fairly self-determined person.

Do you have the courage to label somebody in your very personal analysis as a psychovampire? We often avoid doing so because politeness, getting a grip of yourself and enduring the situation are the very signs that mark us out as victims. Openly admitting to ourselves what we think of someone else is not quite the same thing however as making a psychiatric diagnosis; we're judging on a purely subjective level. In psychotherapy we often experience how the psychovampire, who's often a very close member of the family, is defended by the victim at the rational level with comments like: "He's not as bad as that; he's actually OK otherwise", and "Other people like him a lot". As time goes on though you should be able to form a more neutral judgment for yourself.

CHAPTER 5

Why we experience someone as a psychovampire

*No one is free
who is not master of his own life
(Matthias Claudius, Poet, 1740-1815)*

Most people's initial reaction when identifying the "perpetrator" is to spontaneously confront him in the hope of improving the situation. This is because our first impulse is put the perpetrator out of action and protect the victim from further scrutiny. But in doing so we commit an error of judgment by assuming that this approach is going to change people just because we want them to change. This is not so!

Practice has shown that we must first recognise and understand why people are experienced by some as psychovampires and by others not at all - with the exception of the universal vampires described in Chapter 4. Which "button" does the psychovampire press and what mechanisms does he release in me? The answer to this depends primarily on myself and then on the psychovampire. Though the vampire is determined as a cause of my problems he is first and foremost only the trigger but not the cause of an untreated, subconscious internal conflict which has existed in me for a long time.

Make a distinction between trigger and cause:
the psychovampire is the trigger but not the
cause of an untreated subconscious internal
conflict which has existed in me for a long time.

In Positive Psychotherapy we differentiate between Actual Conflict and Basic Conflict, and Inner Conflict.

Actual conflict is defined as acute or chronic experiences in the present, such as death, career changes, events affecting a partnership, for example, divorce or marriage, financial developments, etc. Actual conflict is initially neutral and its personal significance is directly related to how relevant the experience is for me. Someone dying is primarily a neutral occurrence. It acquires meaning at a personal level through my relationship to the deceased person, my attitude to death and dying, the consequences of the fatality, for example, inheritance issues, and my previous experience with death. The actual conflict may then trigger a dormant basic conflict. In this way, a divorce can reactivate the early loss of a father since it represents the renewed loss of a man that person had loved. Here, the actual conflict opens up an old wound.

The *basic conflict* shows the initial emotional situation which is cemented in my early childhood. An example would be the early loss of a father following the parents' separation and loss of contact to the father. The basic conflict is like a sleeping dog and allows the person to live a normal life at first. You can live for many years, one whole life long, with a basic conflict. In other words, not everybody who has a difficult childhood must have problems later on in life. Only an acute trigger, for example an actual conflict, can reactivate this.

People don't become ill because of a difficult childhood or some current event. There must be a build-up of some *internal conflict*. This happens when different wishes and needs confront each other. It is always an unconscious process and presents an apparently insoluble situation. One frequent consequence can be a feeling of hopelessness and being trapped. The results are mental or physical illness(es). A good example is separation. Current problems with the partner such as unreliability or infidelity bring the talk round to a possible separation. The existence of intrinsic moral concepts, for example, "loyalty until death", which are an integral part of the couple's cultural and educational background, can lead to an insoluble, internal conflict: I can't live with my partner any more but a separation is also out of the question.

The psychovampire reactivates the basic conflict which, as we have established, originates in the early years of childhood. This is exactly where we must begin if we are to achieve long-term "immunization".

The vampire's main point of attack is usually our self-esteem, which forms in childhood, i.e., during the same phase which sees the formation of the basic conflict. The vampire identifies our weak points without deliberate wickedness; how can he when he's unaware of the reasons why he has such control? Positively stated, the vampire helps us to become conscious of our weaknesses and imperfections - unfortunately without us having asked him to do so. It's basically about a sort of free course in self-awareness or self-reflection, which would otherwise take a long time, or never come about.

> Positively speaking, the vampire
> helps us to become
> aware of our weaknesses and
> imperfections as well as our
> doubts and hopes.

The value of self-esteem

Self-esteem under the magnifying glass - Part I:
When you can't say "No"

Ellen (38), marketing assistant, likes her job very much. It's just that she has a problem with her direct superior. Ivan is 32 years old, has been in the company for two years and is very ambitious - with a tendency to be a Snare Vampire. Ellen is conscientious, well-organized and manages her work well - if only Ivan didn't unexpectedly appear in her office so often and give her more new jobs to do. "Ellen, this needs to be settled urgently. I'm sorry, but I've been getting some pressure from the board of directors and have to hand this in by Friday and only you can help me." Ellen comes from a family in which she never learned to say "No". She was always there for others; her personal needs took second place. For the same reason, she's very popular with her colleagues – she's always polite, never complains and does everything she's asked to do. Every time Ivan comes to her office she feels completely drained afterwards, so much so that she inwardly dreads his appearance every day. The work which has given to her so much pleasure – especially when Ivan's predecessor, with whom she got on very well, still worked in the company – is beginning to wear her down. She now has to force herself to go to work every morning (something she never experienced before), she has a cold more often than she used to (in spite of being fit and healthy) and when another job offer comes along she gives notice without really wanting to.

Ivan had pressed the "polite and obliging button", a button which is in very widespread use. 'Polite' here describes the desire to please others, not to burden them, to set aside any personal needs, to saddle yourself with favors for other people and suffer it all in silence. Experience shows that more than 90 percent of psychotherapy patients belong to the polite type who would rather conform than pass the burden to others. It's about a subconscious fear of being rejected or not being loved any more. Individual needs are unconsciously put aside to satisfy the wishes of someone else.

Self-esteem under the magnifying glass - Part II:
"What will people say?"

John (45) is late home from work again. His two children (7 and 8) are still awake but things are pretty quiet. After dinner he brings the children to bed and is just looking forward to a relaxing evening when there's an unexpected ring at the door. His wife Julia answers the door to a friendly couple who were in the neighborhood by chance and thought they'd drop by. "We're not disturbing you, are we? We were close by and just wanted to say hello." Julia comes from a family where they always said: "What will people say if I'm unfriendly or behave badly? You can't do that. What will the neighbours think?" So she lets the guests in although she really doesn't want to and aware that her husband will not be at all pleased. "No, not at all. Come on in. We didn't have anything planned for tonight anyway." A short while later John comes back from the kids' room and the expression on his face is an open book. After some brief small talk he takes leave of his wife and their guests with the excuse that he still has to finish something for work. After the guests have gone, 1 or 2 hours later, Julia goes to the bedroom and is immediately "turned on" by John: "You and your politeness. Why couldn't you tell them they were not wanted? You spoilt the whole evening for us." He turns over and falls asleep. Julia sobs and is angry with herself yet again. Why didn't she turn the visitors away at the door? John would have.

This is all about self-esteem too, something which Julia mostly acquires from outside sources. By satisfying others she gets the recognition she needs, she feels wanted and loved. This frequently leads to problems in relationships. The psychovampires in this example were the guests, without consciously wanting to be. Nor were they aware of the chain reaction they set off.

Each of us has a certain level of self-esteem. But it should be positive. It defines our self-perception and self-assurance but is also the basis for inter-relating with other people. Self-esteem, or the foundation for it, is laid in early childhood. We can't go deeper into the very complicated mechanisms that this involves but there are some factors which contribute substantially to the development of a healthy, or deficient, self-esteem. One determining factor is the question of how parental love was experienced subjectively.

The importance of unconditional love

In psychology we speak of conditional love and unconditional love. Unconditional love is the ideal, though unfortunately, not the norm. Parents love a child simply because it's there. The message, so to speak, is: "You're just what we've been waiting for. You're the child of our dreams. You're exactly what we wanted. You don't need to do or become anything special. The fact that you're here is enough for us." For the child this is a very positive experience and it happily soaks it all up: "It's good that I'm here. I don't have to perform well or behave in a special way." In the first months and years of its life it already recognises how precious it is to be loved. This is the core of a healthy self-esteem which slowly matures and is fed, as it were, from the inside and retained, under normal circumstances, for the rest of a person's life. Perhaps, while you were reading theses lines, you were conscious of a change in your expression, you smiled and had a warm feeling inside, or maybe you were asking yourself if you had experienced any unconditional love from your parents.

The reality of conditional love and the consequences

Far more frequently, parental love is experienced as conditional. Ask parents if they love their child unconditionally and the unequivocal response will be affirmative. In their eyes they have always loved their offspring unconditionally. The important and decisive factor in this is how you or I as a person experienced the love of our parents. Did we feel it? Were we aware of it? Conditional love is often expressed in such familiar terms as: "We love you very much but if you clear up your room, bring good marks home and always keep out of trouble, we will love you even more." This isn't always put into words as such but the toddler already gets an idea of which way the wind blows. Because we all crave for the love of our parents we do everything we can to meet their demands and expectations. As soon as we get to elementary school this mechanism takes on its own momentum. Suddenly performance (school marks) plays a vital role and this sets clear parameters for the future. Such children frequently bring nothing but good results home and later in life they become very successful. But because self-esteem does not come from the inside, they are dependent on a constant "supply" from external sources. Love is generally linked either to achievement and/ or good behaviour (politeness). Decades later, as adults, they are very efficient but they never quite find inner peace of mind; any challenge which, however unconsciously, can lead to increased recognition (and love) is readily accepted. The working environment lends itself well here, especially at a time when society rewards success and achievement.

As we have seen in the case studies, parental vampires, boss vampires or, quite banal, unexpected guests at the front door, all have one thing in common: they appeal to our low self-esteem, "threaten" indirectly to withhold love while promising a reward at the same time: "If you do this for me today, I will love you." And who doesn't want to be loved? Who wants to run the risk of somebody going around and saying something bad about us?

Low self-esteem is therefore a frequent reason for falling into the clutches of a psychovampire and expresses itself though an increased desire for love from outside or in the inability to say No and the wish to please everyone. Of course, there are also situations which are not in themselves about self-esteem but where other personal causes play a role. These are situations in which we feel unfairly treated; situations in which someone gives us the run around or lets us walk into a trap; when we sense anger and aggression in the other person but this person doesn't verbalize his feelings; unspoken hypocrisy, emotions and problems; when someone fails to meet our expectations; people who dramatize minor situations; people who waste their time on unnecessary details and problems. It goes without saying that all of these are always subjective experiences.

Exercise for analyzing self-esteem

The following technique is taken from management training and is used the check personal self-esteem.

Each of us possesses 100 % self-esteem. In corporate terms this is the same as having 100 % self-esteem shares. The question is: who really owns my self-esteem shares? To whom or what have I subconsciously surrendered my self-esteem or part of it? Is there even a main shareholder who owns more than 50 % and therefore controls my self-esteem? Do I still hold any shares myself or have I surrendered everything? Dozens of seminars in which the exercise was conducted have shown how extremely difficult this assignment is – because it goes very deep. But it's a very important step towards a self-determined and full life. To reach this I must first determine who or what influences my well-being and my self-esteem. Only then I can start to make changes.

Now try to divide the 100 percent self-esteem in different categories. Most of them will involve a person; but they may also be things like health or money.

> If we compare ourselves to a corporation
> each of us has 100 % self-esteem shares
> The question is: who is the owner of
> these self-esteem shares?

Just how dependent we are on this thing or person can easily be established by a countercheck. How is your self-esteem influenced when you are ill or if you were ill? What influence does a quarrel with your partner have on your self-esteem, or a problem at work?

A word on the main shareholder: There *can* be one, but there doesn't have to be.

A word about "I": You can own a portion of your self-esteem shares yourself but be prepared to answer the critical question: Is this really so? Sometimes we're only content with ourselves if we're successful (career) or our relationship (contact) is going well. To possess my own shares means that I accept myself as I am and that there's a part of me which exists independently of my performance or other factors. You can compare this to the gold reserves in the Central Bank or Fort Knox.

The result is often not only astonishing but also depressing at first. Quite often we have no idea at all who or what influences us. Then suddenly it becomes clear why I experience a certain person (or thing) as a psychovampire – their not inconsiderable influence on my self-esteem. This is the starting point for a positive change: I consciously decide who I want to give my self-esteem shares to and who not to. It is, after all, my "company", in other words, my life.

How can I improve my self-esteem?

People often complain that they have achieved nothing. Everything has been insignificant: "What have I done so far? Anybody could have done that." A successful technique to avoid this is to create of a list of previous achievements, successes, performances, crises survived, etc. This list is initially drawn up with the help of the therapist or coach. At home the client then complements the list on their own and brings it to the next session. At first, many find it very difficult to make a longer list; this is mainly due to our tendency to stick to the traditional CV-style (title, qualifications, positions, etc.). But now we're more concerned with the *emotional CV* – a very personal and unique list. Nobody knows what I have gone through.

For example, how hard it is for me to remain in the family for the sake of the children although my partner is making my life hell. In the column 'marital status' in the conventional, rational CV you'll only find the word 'married', but in the emotional one it will say how difficult it is, what it means for me on a day to day basis. etc. Suddenly you are forced to acknowledge how much you actually have achieved up to now, what you have gone through, without anyone else necessarily knowing about it. We realize that we are capable of many achievements and this raises our self-esteem – continuously and with lasting effect.

Exercise: Creating an emotional CV

Using the following criteria create your own emotional CV which is personal and which you mustn't show to anyone:

- Challenges mastered
- Crises survived
- Conflicts solved
- Problems 'overcome'
- 'Insoluble' situations endured

Case study 1: A 45-year-old mother of three, whose husband is editor-in-chief of a big American newspaper, comes to treatment because she's suffering from bouts of angst and depression. In addition to many early childhood and current problems, one of her recurring themes is that she does nothing while her husband goes out to work and earns the money. With the therapist's help she tries to make a "success list", the key to success lying in the breakdown of single events. The three children are broken down into: became pregnant three times (more than 25 percent of all married couples today remain unintentionally childless, so becoming pregnant is in itself already quite a success story); three pregnancies "delivered", three births survived, childhood illnesses, kindergarten, school, etc.

Case study 2: A successful 28-year-old businessman with sleeping disturbances and fears of failure was also encouraged to draw up a list and felt reassured and exonerated when he added up everything he'd achieved up to that point. One example will indicate this: in therapy he spoke at length of the fact that as a young man he'd gone to Moscow straight after finishing his studies. He regarded this as perfectly normal, and entered it on his list as an event of little import ("anybody could do that"). Yet when he and the therapist analyzed how many of his study colleagues had actually done it, how many foreigners can't take the life in Russia and in some instances, leave the country for good again after only 48 hours (!) and that he had already been there for four years, he began to realize and appreciate his achievements. He was also able to liberate himself from the "Himalayas Phenomenon" (comp. Chapter 3: The Himalayas Vampire). At the age of 28 he had already chalked up some remarkable experiences and achievements and, more importantly, also learnt to be proud of them.

Psychodynamically speaking, apart from the Himalayas phenomenon, this is all about the ability to accept compliments, enjoy personal success and share it with others, praise yourself and be proud of yourself - all the things we were brought up to believe were not the done thing and were seen as sure signs of egoistic behaviour.

CHAPTER 6

A therapeutic side note: Self-help with Positive Psychotherapy

This is the highest wisdom that I own; freedom and life are earned by those alone who conquer them each day anew.

(Goethe)

In many a therapy session the one topic which repeatedly comes up is relationships: relationships with others and with oneself. "Why doesn't this person like me? Why does she reject me? I let my boss take advantage of me again and he's worn me down with his remarks. My wife says I'm as bad as her father".

Some of the basic strategies and techniques of positive psychotherapy can help us to understand the influence of psychovampires and protect us against them long term.

Positive Psychotherapy (PPT), which was developed by Prof. Dr. Nossrat Peseschkian in 1977, is a humanistic-psychodynamic psychotherapy method. Positive Psychotherapy can be applied in different areas of life: in therapy, consultation, coaching, management training, education and prevention - and to promote intercultural understanding. It is essentially based on three main principles: hope, balance and self-help. In the following pages these are briefly explained and their significance in dealing with psychovampires is illustrated. (Note: Positive Psychotherapy by Nossrat Peseschkian (1977) and Positive Psychology by Martin Seligman (1998) are separate approaches which have different goals and missions. See also: Theo A. Cope "Positive Psychotherapy: Let the Truth be Told". International Journal of Psychotherapy: 2014, Vol. 18, No.2, pp. 62-71)

Hope

The concept of the Positive refers in principle to the fact that Positive Psychotherapy is not only aimed at removing a certain symptom or disorder (symptom-oriented medicine), but that the first step is to try and discover the meaning of the illness and to make the sufferer aware of its significance. Positive here refers back to the original meaning of actual, real (Latin: positum, positivus). Actual and real are not only the problems and conflicts a person or family is going through; they are also the ability to handle these conflicts, to learn from them and to be cured as a result. Illness can also be defined as the ability to react this way and not that way to a situation or a conflict. It always involves an attempt at self-healing by the individual affected, which is then more or less successful. Patients suffer not only from their disorders and illnesses they also experience hopelessness, which is transferred to them through the diagnosis. Positive Psychotherapy is a resource-oriented approach in psychotherapy which primarily looks at the possibilities of the affected person and only then deals with the illness. Its concept of mankind encompasses, among other things, the essential elements found in humanistic psychology, for example, the acceptance of a person's ability to change, since therapeutic treatment would be pointless if it wasn't supported by the conviction that people can change. Positive Psychotherapy assumes that man actively shapes his own existence, that he consciously or unconsciously orients himself on certain values, seeks to give his existence some meaning and that self-realization can only be attained through constant interaction with one's social environment.

The 'positive action' in Positive Psychotherapy results from the positive image of man underlying the statement that every person - without exception – possesses two inherent abilities: the ability to love and the cognitive faculty. Both these basic abilities are innate to every human and invested in him from birth. Depending on his environment (upbringing, education and culture) and the time in which he lives (zeitgeist), these basic faculties can develop differently and lead to a unique and unmistakable structure of traits which form a person's character and uniqueness. The concept of core faculties means that the person is fundamentally good. 'Fundamentally good' means that each of us comes equipped with a range of skills which need to be developed, comparable to the potential waiting to break out of a seed.

In practice this positive image of man means that we begin by accepting ourselves and others as we are, but also see what we can become. This involves treating the individual - with all his problems and illnesses - as a person in order to then become more closely acquainted with the human skills which have until that moment remained unknown, hidden and buried by the illness. Disorders and illnesses are therefore regarded as a kind of ability to react to a certain conflict in one way and not in another. In this sense, Positive Psychotherapy reinterprets the symptoms and disorders.

Some clinical conditions are stated here as examples:

- *Depression* is the ability to react to conflicts with deepest emotionality.
- *Fear of loneliness* means to have the basic need to be together with other people.
- *Alcoholism* is the ability to supply yourself with the warmth (and love) which you do not receive from others.

One consequence of this is that positive action in Positive Psychotherapy leads to a new perception of all involved - patient, family and psychotherapist – and this forms the basis for future therapeutic cooperation. It allows a forceful dialogue with existing problems and conflicts. This approach helps to focus on the 'real' patient and to make conflicts 'visible' which are otherwise concealed and about whose existence the patient is generally unaware. The real patient often sits at home while the symptom bearer comes to therapy. This is also a reason why more women visit a therapist and is in no way an indication that they are more in need of treatment than men.

The principle of hope helps us to reflect on our own inner (self-) worth, even in difficult situations, and gives us the confidence that change is possible and that I have the ability to cope with the present situation. And it is exactly this hope that releases forces and energies which are so vital in the battle with psychovampires.

Balance

Research by N. Peseschkian in different cultures has shown that there are four areas of life in which we can invest our energy, which give us self-esteem and which can also be termed 'The four qualities of life':

- Body and health (body)
- Career and achievement (mind)
- Relationships and contacts (heart)
- Future and meaning (soul)

This balance model is based on the holistic concept of the human being in Positive Psychotherapy. We speak in this connection of biological-physical, rational-intellectual, socio-emotional and mental-spiritual spheres and abilities in a person. Although we all have the potential for all four abilities in us, some of them are specially accentuated by environment and socialization, while others are neglected. Every person develops his own preferences with regard to how he processes conflicts as they happen ('Four methods of processing conflict'): escape into physical complaints and illnesses, escape into work, escape into loneliness or sociability, or escape into fantasy. Which forms of conflict management we choose depends essentially on our learning experiences, above all, on those we were able to make in childhood. Positive Psychotherapy teaches us that it's not the person who is healthy that has no problems but the one that has learnt to deal appropriately with conflicts as they appear. Healthy, according to the balance model, is the person who tries to divide his energy resources evenly in all four areas. One aim of consultation or psychotherapeutic treatment is to help the client /

patient to recognise his own resources and to mobilize them with the aim of creating a dynamic balance between the four areas. Special value is placed on a balanced energy spread ('25 percent' for each area) and not on an even time distribution. A one-sidedness which persists uncorrected over a longer period of time can, in addition to other causes, lead to conflicts and, logically, disorders. In this connection it's vital to accept that the uniqueness of the person be taken into consideration. In this way he can arrive at an individual balance within the four areas which is consistent with his needs. While in the individualistic cultures of Western Europe and North America the spheres of physical health and sport (body) and career (achievement) play a predominant role, in the collectivist cultures of the Orient (Middle East) the prevailing areas are family, friends and guests (contacts), as well as questions about the future, the meaning of life and ideological questions (imagination / intuition).

Preventive check according to the balance model

The balance model can help us in manifold ways to become stronger in the four areas of Body, Mind, Heart and Soul and so enable us to protect ourselves better against psychovampires.

Use the following questions for self-examination and self-reflection to become more aware of how your personal balance model should look and where your priorities lie. The questions refer to your current status but they're also intended to help you understand your own predilections. This explains the questions on your childhood.

Questions on Body

What physical disorder are you suffering from?
How much and what do you smoke or drink?
Do you pay attention to a well-balanced diet?
Do you take time for meals, sport and relaxation?
How important to you are your body and your appearance? Do you listen to your body or does it just have to function?
Do you suffer from the following disorders: sleeping problems, restlessness, difficulties in concentration, constant fatigue?

How does your body react to trouble, stress, shortage of time, conflicts, worries, criticism, great pleasure?

Do you like your body?

What importance had and has tenderness and sexuality in the relationship of your parents to each other and to you? And how is it in your current partnership?

Questions on Achievement

Are you happy with your career?

Does your job provide enough security, income and recognition?

How many hours do you work daily / weekly? Do you feel overworked?

Are you afraid of failure?

Do you get on with your colleagues and superiors?

How do you react when your performance is criticized?

Do you feel good even when you have nothing to do?

If you had enough money, would you still work?

How important is your job to you for your self-esteem?

Which activity would you enjoy performing?

What did you have to do earlier to be loved by your parents and win their approval: Good marks? Keep out of trouble?

Questions on Contact

Are you happy with your partnership? If not, why?

Which of you is the more outgoing, you or your partner?

How much time do you spend with your partner, family, friends?

How is your relationship with your parents? Is there a person you can talk to about anything, even the most intimate problems?

Did you have many contacts as a child, or were you isolated?

Do you feel put under pressure by your social connections and obligations?

Do you spend a lot of time thinking about what the other people think or say about you?

Do you lack social contacts and emotional warmth?

Do you need people round you, or can you also spend a lot of time by yourself?

Questions on Imagination and future

With do you think about most (e.g., health, job, relationship, family)?
Do you think about dying and death?
What do you think happens to you after death?
Do you sometime ask yourself about the meaning of life?
What convictions or religious beliefs did your parents live by?
What makes life and staying healthy worthwhile?
What would you like to achieve or change in the next five years?
Which is the most urgent change?
What would you do if you had no more problems?
What is your most ardent wish?

The less I find myself in balance, the more likely it is that somebody or something can unbalance me. So I experience a psychovampire as much more menacing if he appeals to an area of life from which I draw my entire self-esteem. Looked at differently: by attaining an internal and external balance in the four areas of the balance model, we create an invulnerable shell which a psychovampire will find hard to pierce.

Self-help

Within the framework of psychotherapy and self-help, Positive Psychotherapy applies a 5-stage procedure which is broken down into the following units: observation and dissociation, compiling an inventory, situative encouragement, verbalization and goal extension. This 'strategy' is applied over the full course of therapy as well as during one-off sessions and as a self-help technique.

Stage of Observation and Distancing

The aim of this stage in the therapeutic process is to take stock and analyze the patient's / client's situation. It should help him to move from an abstract level to a concrete, descriptive one. The patient expresses (in writing if possible) what or who has made him angry, whom he experiences as psychovampire, when his symptoms increase and/or he gets into conflict with others. At this level a process of learning to differentiate commences. The patient starts to isolate the conflict and describe it in more detail. By becoming an observer he dissociates himself more and more from his own conflict situation and this leads to an expansion of the initial 'neurotic constriction'. In this way the patient becomes the observer of himself and his environment.

Stage of Inventory

At a therapeutic session or during consultation, the main aim is to clarify the learning past and to make the basic reasoning behind the concepts and misunderstandings transparent for the patient. Situations which to the patient appear largely unchangeable and personality-related are relativized in the context of their autobiographical preconditions. With the help of an inventory of the actual abilities (socialization norms), we determine in which behavioral areas the patient and his conflict partner possess positive or negative qualities. For psychovampires it's all about exposing this and recognizing which "button" they press and what this has to do with the patient.

Stage of Situational Encouragement

In order to build up a bond of trust with the conflict partner, the patient learns how to strengthen certain positively defined qualities in the other person and to be aware of the corresponding critically defined qualities in his own character. Instead of constantly criticizing the conflict partner the patient learns to encourage him, basing his actions on the experiences from the first and second steps. Together with the therapist he tries to discover some positive aspects about the psychovampire, even if the only one is that he helps us recognise our weak points.

Stage of Verbalization

To get away from the speechlessness or linguistic distortion of the conflict, communication with the conflict partner is practiced step by step according to agreed guidelines. Once a bond of trust has been built up in the third step, and open communication is possible, one can now speak about the positive and negative qualities and experiences. At this stage it often comes to an open and constructive debate for the first time in years. This level also introduces the patient to some of the techniques and rules of communication.

Stage of Broadening of Goals

The Target Development Level accompanies the patient from the outset. He is asked to consider the question: "What do I do when I don't have these problems any longer? What do I do after I have got rid of the psychovampire and have more energy again?" This stage also has a preventive character to help avoid 'a pressure release situation' after 'successful' therapy. The patient learns to gradually detach himself from his therapist and develop new abilities that he neglected in the past, for whatever reason. Micro-targets and macro-targets are developed together with the therapist.

As an encouraging example to put into practice with Positive Psychotherapy here is the written reflection of a patient on reaching the end of her therapy:

The luminous colours

There was once a gray chameleon who went to a psychotherapist and asked him for help.

The therapist asked: "How did you get to become a gray chameleon?" The chameleon explained that it had always behaved in the way expected of it or in the way it imagined that was expected. That's why it was constantly under great pressure and, to make matters worse, it had also lost its personality and style.

At the beginning of the therapy the chameleon was gray – it was sad, weak, low in spirits and very desperate. It was extremely unhappy because it was on the verge of destroying its home, its body and its soul and also the soul of the fox with whom it lived together in the foreign country – and with it he would lose a precious relationship.

The therapist asked many questions and listened carefully. Appropriate remarks at the right moment helped the chameleon recognise that deep down there still slumbered many colours and not just the sad gray. The chameleon had accepted the role of little mouse as an alternative. But even this new role didn't bring all its abilities to the fore and could not reactivate all the colours that would help it cement a stable partnership with the fox and lead them to a full and happy life with a family and satisfying careers.

It was a difficult time and a challenging task for the chameleon, but also for those close to him and for the brilliant doctor. In silent accord, the therapist also changed his own colours during the course of the therapy. In order to help the tired, gray chameleon, the therapist had to become aggressive. He attacked the chameleon to coax it from its shell. And so it learnt to be black and absolutely sad and, when it was angry, to turn green. The therapist supported the learning chameleon with a constant series of stories and questions and his remarkable talent for listening patiently.

The chameleon slowly began to grasp his concepts and made efforts not to copy other people as its role models any more. It understood that it was unique and could choose its own distinctive colour blending and that it could and should learn through observation. It rejected the idea of copying its mother and lived from that time onwards more at peace with itself. It became more authentic and before long it wasn't a chameleon any more in the original sense of the word.

It's hard to say what sort of animal it became. Whatever it was, it had become a real and more stable personality. It could deal with reality and from then on was yellow when active, light blue when quietly watching and, when listening, was white with concentration. It could turn green when upset and be able to communicate constructively. In an emotional state it could be pink and ultimately was able to unite all the different color tones to a mixture of differing intensity according to each situation.

With his multicolor therapy the therapist had given back to the once gray chameleon all its brilliant and subdued colours. The chameleon radiated happiness and gratitude. It wanted ….. to give away all the colours and joys of this world and wrap everybody in positive thoughts…

CHAPTER 7

Preventive measures and immunization techniques

I'm a pessimist in the present,
but an optimist for the future
(Wilhelm Busch)

Now that we've learned the psychological mechanisms of psychovampirism, the question poses itself as to how we can benefit from this knowledge and so protect ourselves permanently from the people who suck our energy away.

External influence versus self-determination

It's not situations that weigh us down; it's our attitudes towards them that decide how we react. Situations are always experienced by us as stressful and exhausting if we have the (subjective) feeling that we're being manipulated by an extraneous force. By this we mean that somebody else is doing something to us, without us wanting them to. The same situation or task is experienced in an absolutely different way depending on whether I do it voluntarily (self-determined) or whether I have to do it (external influence). A good example are children: if we tell them they should clear up their room in the evening, there's opposition and a whole lot more. If we say they can watch TV after they've cleared up their room, they run to their rooms and nothing can stop them. With adults it's the same, at home, at work or at the week-end.

The psychovampire makes us feel that we are being uncontrollably influenced from outside: he or she drains our energy, changes our mood and can sometimes even change our whole life. Our lives are lived for us and we do not live any more. We feel as though we're in the 'wrong' film; unfortunately, this film happens to be a live broadcast, i.e., there's no way to reverse it – it's the film of our life!

To improve stress management and energy management we should write down all the situations in which we feel manipulated and analyze why we feel this way and what can we do to change it. The following check list helps to analyze the causes for your particular external influence. Please answer the following questions:

a. When do you feel that your life is not under your own control?
1) In which situations (early morning traffic jam, etc.)?
2) With which people (boss, partner, parents-in-law, ex-partners, children…)?
3) For which tasks that you have to do or are assigned to (when your boss or partner asks you to do something)?

b. What could be the reason?
1) The 'person with the request', because you do not get on well with him/her?
2) The task itself, because something has changed and you do not agree with the changes?

c. *You'd like to change something* but you are prevented from implementing your ideas and just have to put up with waiting (e.g., in a lengthy conference or discussion)?

Immunization

Now that the vampires have been exposed and analyzed and with their help I have recognised my weak points and, hopefully, processed them (a weakness I know about is no longer a weakness!), we can turn to immunization.

Immunization against psychovampires is primarily a matter of changing our own perceptions. If your efforts show no results, you should probably consider changing your job or personal situation. The latter option is difficult especially in a family structure or often hardly feasible because life tends to become more complicated with increasing age. Situations are also dependent on each other, while the perception of them depends solely on my attitude. Consequently, it lies in my own hands if I want to change a situation which is causing me stress. I can do this by thinking about my own attitude towards it, then question it and finally try to make changes.

Sometimes I can simply get rid of the vampire by reducing contact to a minimum or avoiding him completely, telling myself: "Why should I do this to myself?" We sometimes refuse to let go of relationships when we could and should easily cut them off.

Group and individual contacts

Some psychovampires are easy to get on with when they're alone. Others are better to deal with in a group. Some are surprisingly weak when they're on their own and, like a sort of ringleader, need a group around them. Others are unbearable when alone.

The solo dancers

Imagine an aunt or your mother-in-law wins a weekend trip to a health resort and invites you to come along as her companion. You already know that the train journey is going to be hell, let alone several days when you won't be able to avoid her, and be forced to listen to her constant talking. At family reunions though this same aunt is quite bearable because you only have to exchange a few brief words with her and can then devote your attention to someone less strenuous.

Some time ago Vincent P. went abroad on business and was accompanied by a colleague with whom every second seemed like an hour. It was quite an ordeal. During these torturous hours he swore never again to go away with this person and to avoid such draining experiences in future. Ever since then it's worked. Vincent has regular contact with this colleague but avoids any prolonged personal encounter - and so the relationship functions well. Of course, the situation is not resolved but, in this case, it's neither possible nor necessary as long as Vincent keeps the vampire at a distance.

The hordes

Some vampires are very dangerous in groups; at work, for example, where they create a negative atmosphere and apply various manipulation techniques. Vampires can often be heard reeling out same the old chestnuts: "We've always done it that way", "Anyone could do that", When you've been here as long as I have, you'll understand how things are done here," "The youth of today," etc. Arguing with these people in front of or in a group is 'lethal'. The only way out is not to overreact and suggest a one-to-one talk at a later date. Here's a good example:

During a lecture a young man puts his hand up and, in front of all the 100 or so in the audience, tells the speaker: "With reference to what you've just been saying, we've heard it all before. It's nothing new. I thought you'd be telling us something we didn't already know."

The lecturer interprets these remarks as an open provocation and each of the 100 or so listeners is, of course, waiting with baited breath for his reaction. The psychovampire in the listener's group expects the speaker to deal with the provocation right there in front of the group. It doesn't matter what the speaker says in reply - he won't be able to 'take this vampire down' in the group because the group is protecting him consciously or, as is more likely in this scenario, unconsciously. And that's the reason why he uses the group as a protective shield.

A good off-the-cuff answer to disarm the vampire in front of before his audience would, for example, be:

"Thank you for your thoughts" - and leave the troublemaker high and dry. Then again, you could also say: "Thank you very much. What do the others think?" The other listeners then frequently defend the speaker. But this variation can last longer and develop a momentum which the speaker may not want at that precise moment.

You can also say: "Why don't you come and see me after my presentation and we'll have more time to discuss this." Most don't come at all and if they do then they're vampires who, once isolated, present no danger. Ideally, you can use the opportunity to get the Psychovampire alone and put him through the "mangle".

Learn to distinguish which psychovampires are easier to lead in the group and which in a one-to-one context. The same person can be a completely different experience for us if we look at the context in which we meet him or confront him.

Vampire themes to avoid at your peril

There are certain topics which should not be brought up in the presence of particular psychovampires. Compare it to a balancing act on a tightrope 300 feet in the air, and without a safety wire: a wrong word, a wrong topic - and you're lost and at the psychovampire's mercy.

Avoiding gasbags

A female colleague who never stops talking should never be offered the 'H' question ('How are you?') as this only releases the flood gates to a 30-minute discourse.

- A much better opener is: "It's great to see you again."
- Just don't ask her how she is!

Protect your emotions from possible Vampire situations

More difficult to deal with are emotional issues such as the effects of long-term unemployment, the period after separation or divorce, or bereavement, etc. If you're in such a difficult situation or phase and this is a sensitive area for you, avoid a conversation with certain people - potential vampires - who are bound to ask you how you're feeling.

Example 1:

A 30-year-old patient, who'd been studying for 12 years without taking his degree, sought the help of a psychotherapist. A class reunion was soon to take place. The therapist advised the patient to steer clear of this gathering as he was afraid that his former classmates would see him as a failure. At some point they would inevitably ask him about his career - expecting to hear the usual stories about 'my house, my job, my yacht, etc'. The patient stayed at home and was more than pleased that he did.

Example 2:

You're separated and no one else knows about it yet. Whenever someone asks: 'Isn't your husband here today?', you should have a good answer ready, otherwise the unsuspecting questioner, who could just be a vampire for you in this particular situation, might trigger a whole bundle of emotions in you. With the right answer you steel yourself against unwanted 'attacks'.

- Identify your sensitive topics.
- Avoid people who bring them up in the conversation, repeatedly or in certain situations.
- Avoid places where these issues can be talked about / brought up.
- Prepare a good standard answer in advance, if you already know that the question might be posed. Then you can answer without great emotional involvement.

Psychovampire statements invariably affect us more than we think even think though we never stop to wonder if this person has a sound judgment and understands the situation emotionally and professionally, in other words, is qualified to make such statements (analogous to the cases of the Expert Vampire).

Mr. Peter is an entrepreneur and has to dismiss some of his staff. He's very concerned about what the redundant employees and others say about him. A few of the remaining staff talk to him and give him a bad conscience ("Why have you fired these people?" etc.). His brother, who works for the company but has never run his own business, says that he'd have done everything different. Just as in the case study of the Expert Vampire in Chapter 3, the only person qualified to make decisions about redundancy is somebody who knows what it's like be responsible for other people or even manages his own business - and he/she would never interfere because human resource management is a constant theme for CEOs.

- Ask yourself if the personal opinions of critics are at all important to you and cause you to examine your own assessment?
- Do you ask yourself: "What will people say?"

If you can answer questions with a 'No', then other people's opinions are like water off a duck's back to you.

The most dangerous thing you can do is to defend and justify yourself, or go into long explanations, because your opposite just won't understand what you're trying to say.

If even words fail to hit home, imagine that you have stamped the letters PV on the psychovampire's forehead every time you expose one for yourself. You may not be able to avoid meeting this person on a daily basis but always imagine the PV stamp or a cap with the PV logo on it and inwardly take up an active defense position. That way you can no longer be attacked so easily.

General immunization through energy balance

General protection, which acts like a universal immunization is achieved through a balanced energy distribution, i.e. a balance between wish und reality. The energy distribution model as presented by Nossrat Peseschkian and explained in detail in the previous chapter assumes the need to divide energy distribution between the four qualities of life: 'body - mind – heart - soul. This concept allows for a wide range of applications and possible variations. Three therapy techniques are described in brief below and are active at the levels of energy, time and wish:

1. Energy: the client is requested to record his energy distribution for that day in the four areas described on page 125. The only requirement is that he doesn't exceed a life energy total of 100 percent. The client's self-assessment should be purely subjective.
2. Time: the client should specify a division of time for the four areas. How much time does he invest each day in each of the individual areas? Here again, a subjective self-assessment is essential.
3. Wish: how should my life be? How much energy would I like to invest in each of the four areas if the decision was up to me?

Possible interpretation: in the 'best case' all three models are identical, i.e. today I live the way I want; and areas which require a great deal of time are allocated a corresponding amount of energy. Quite often though, this is not what happens. More often than not, there's a considerable difference between energy expenditure and time distribution. This can be interpreted as a sign that a problem or conflict exists in a sphere of life with a large energy input but where little time is invested. This is almost always the case in relationship issues: an hour at home costs as much energy and effort as a whole day at work.

As psychovampires practically only attack our self-esteem we can use these three techniques to great effect as preventive measures to ward off attacks.

CHAPTER 8

Dealing with Emergency Vampire Situations

If you want understand life,
don't believe what people say and write.
Observe yourself instead, and make your own thoughts.
(A. P. Chekhov, 1860–1904, Russian poet)

Psychovampires seems to possess an innate ability for appearing uninvited and, above all, unexpected – and more often than not when we can't escape or defend ourselves. We've already discussed this mechanism; it's about the difficulty to say No or, put another way, the fear of disappointing someone. It's particularly valid in situations where a decision must be taken very quickly and there is, as it were, no time to think, that we fall into the psychovampire's clutches. Here are some thoughts and tips for acute cases of psychovampirism.

Phone attack

We've all been there: the phone rings, you answer it unthinkingly and are immediately faced with a lightning decision: the relatives want to come by and this doesn't suit your plans at all; a colleague wants to come over to your office right away to clear something up; a friend wants you to come to a party you don't want to go to. Experience shows that someone who sees himself as a victim is hard put to say No immediately and set limits. You can (and must) learn to do this, but it is very difficult, and time-consuming. In such an 'acute vampire emergency' only one thing helps right off: play for time. Make a firm resolution to win some time whenever you receive sudden phone calls. For example, say: "Can I call you back in five minutes? I have to check my diary and I haven't got it here." Or: "I'll have to ask my partner first and see what his plans are. What number can I call back in a few minutes?" These delaying tactics are a simple but very effective strategy. Once you've put the phone down you have plenty of time to consider the options. In these emergency situations you are fully exonerated if you resort to the occasional white lie in order to gain time and think through your reply.

Ad hoc raids

The unexpected moment of attack is a typical psychovampire technique and it comes in different shapes and sizes, as these four examples show:

Example 1:
It's the office party and your boss comes up to you and asks for your assistance in a current project over the next few days: "Miller, come to my office on Monday morning so we can discuss this."

Example 2:
Mother-in-law calls and complains that she's all alone and no one loves her: "I know you all have a lot do and my problems aren't so important. Maybe it'd be better if I wasn't here anymore. Nobody would miss me anyway."

Example 3:
Susan's partner makes a silly joke at her cost in front of all her guests: "Come on Susan, smile, and don't look so serious. Forget work for a moment. Let yourself go."

Example 4:

The parents of a teenage boy who wants to go out in the evening with his friends say: "We don't think it's a good idea if you go out with Jake and his friends this evening. They're not the right company for you. If you really want to go, you can, but we're not happy about it. You'll see."

Due to the complexity and diversity of psychovampires there's no silver bullet solution to ad-hoc-attacks, only to individual strategies.

What to do in emergencies

Tip No. 1: When in doubt, say No. This is almost always useful in vampire situations.

Example 1:

You're in a store and thinking of buying a new tablet. The sales assistant has a special deal and is doing his best to persuade you to buy it. After 15 minutes' persuasive sales talk he succeeds and you purchase the tablet. But even before you get to the checkout you have the feeling that you really wanted to buy something else. Sound familiar? Experience shows that it's best to say No if you're in any doubt. It's better to go into town again on another day, better to call someone back later, better to apologize - anything is better than just to say Yes and be annoyed with yourself later when you realize what you've done.

> There are few situations in life
> when we kick ourselves in retrospect
> because we didn't grab the opportunity –
> but there are countless ones when we
> very much regret having said Yes and
> ignoring the protests of our inner voice.

Example 2:

Kim (35 years old, secretary) remembers her great moment in the registry office: "I was at the Registry Office 15 years ago and the officer asked me if I wanted to take this man in marriage and I really wanted to say No. My heart was beating so loudly that I was afraid the others could hear it. But then I said to myself I can't say No now. What would everyone think? I felt sorry for my fiancé too and all the relatives waiting behind us so full of expectation, not to mention all the invited guests. I couldn't send them all home. So I said Yes. But our marital problems began soon after the wedding and the result was that I got divorced a year ago and now have to bring up two small children. I should have 'No' when I had the chance."

> Paradoxically, we tend to devote
> a lot of time to relatively minor matters –
> like buying handbags or a smart phone.
> But on such momentous decisions like
> choosing the right partner or career we
> waste relatively little thought because
> social pressure and the expectations of
> others force us into making decisions.

Tip 2: Check which button the Psychovampire has pressed.

Making use of a short period to reflect and consider is often enough to make me see why my opposite number has caught me on the wrong foot again. Ask yourself the following questions:

-   Which button has the vampire pressed?
-   Which weakness has he/she detected in me?
-   Has he appealed to my low self-esteem?
-   Has he criticized my appearance, something which bothers me too, after I put on a few pounds?
-   Has he reopened old wounds?
-   Has he tried to make me feel sorry for him?

Tip 3: Arm yourself with words.

As intimated in the section "Avoiding the gasbags" (*see page 140 in German version),* affirmative comments are a safe way to ward off danger in advance.

Since it's always the same vulnerable points that others exploit we'd do well to think up some answers or ripostes and have them ready to hand in an emergency and so not be fully unprepared. With pro-active comments we keep the upper hand and the cut remains superficial. For example:

Women who are also successful managers are used to hearing the line: "Typical woman", and rightly take offence; they can also think about where it's coming from and, even though it still needs to be swallowed for what it is, can come up with a good proactive response: "You probably expected a man instead of me and I'm sorry to disappoint you but I'm sure that we'll be able to work well together today."

Answering and reacting with proverbs, sayings or words of wisdom likewise comes under the 'affirmative remarks' category. This way you take the proactive lead and can steer the course of the encounter. It also prevents a head to head between the two antagonists and the remark becomes a kind of mediator, sometimes even a buffer.

Two examples of lecture scenarios:

A) You're in the middle of a presentation and someone arrives late, struggles through the rows of seats and causes a minor disturbance in the room. Since the audience has now diverted its attention to the latecomer, why not use the scene proactively? You could, for example, say: *"You're not late. We started early."*

B) You're giving a lecture and after about an hour some people leave the room. In most cases your self-confidence begins to waver. This is because you make the mistake of forgetting the other 90 percent of the audience who still want to listen. Instead you inwardly agonize those who have lefts, asking yourself: "Was my presentation that boring? Didn't they like it? Why did they go?". You notice a certain unrest pervading the room and that a break would be appropriate, even if you weren't planning one. At this moment you could make the following proposal: "We all know how increasingly important the work-life balance is becoming and so, after you've all been so attentive, what do you say to a short break? *Would you prefer an Oriental or a Western break? You know the difference?"* Then briefly explain that in the West five-minute breaks really are five minutes, in areas further south they could turn into 10 to 15 minutes. "What kind of break would you prefer?". This shifts the responsibility to the audience and you find out if the need for a break applies to the majority or if the participants who left the room were an isolated case. As the saying goes: 'He who asks, leads'.

Direct attack is the best form of defense. Either you lead proactively or you will be led reactively. And: he who asks, leads!

Proverbs are a particularly effective counter-attack in the face of tasteless comments.

Tina is 39 years old and about to get married (finally). Hardly anyone in her circle of friends and family expected her to find a partner at 'her age'. On the day of the wedding she's beleaguered by distant relatives and friends who come up to her and say: "Well, so you finally found someone. We'd already given up hope." Should she now explain herself and tell them her whole life story so far? If you find yourself surrounded by a whole pack of psychovampires often the only thing that helps is to take the bull by the horns: How about a Chinese proverb: "The teacher arrives when the student is ready. Now you can consider which of us, my husband or I, is the student and which the teacher." By the time the vampires have digested this proverb and transferred it to the situation, Tina has already moved on - and leaves the pack standing there dumfounded.

Desperate measures: When nothing else works, consciously take on the role of psychovampire for your opposite and beat him at his own game.

By now you'll have learned how to suck a person dry, how to get him into a position where he'll do what you want.

CHAPTER 9

Self-analysis: the psychovampire test

"For many people it is easier to suffer, than to change something." (old saying)

Am I easy prey for vampires?

We've established that psychovampires can strike 'anytime and anywhere'. It's therefore worth asking ourselves, as a preventive measure and to be clear in our own minds, to what extent we're easy prey for vampires and if we're a typical or less typical or just a one-off victim, or do we send out 'signals' which the vampires pick up.

Do you sometimes catch yourself wondering:
'Why do these vampires come to ME? There are so many other people out there.'
'Why do I attract difficult people?'
'All the men (or women) I get to know have problems or are already taken.'
'Why do I always get such difficult bosses?'
'This always happens to me. What am I doing wrong?'
'I'm dogged by bad luck.'
'They always leave me feeling drained.'
'They stick to me like glue..'

'I feel like a wastepaper basket. Everybody dumps their garbage here.'

If these statements sound familiar, you're a potential victim or easy prey for vampires! Just having these questions circle around in your head is enough to send out the special signals which reflect a basic attitude in the acceptance of your role as a victim. It all happens in the subconscious. As part of your self-analysis and as a way out of the victim mentality you must become consciously aware of these signals.

'What signals do I send?' Or: 'When am I most susceptible to psychovampires?'

Try to answer the following questions honestly:

Questions

1. How do I rate my self-esteem?
2. Am I often plagued by self-doubt?
3. Do I have weaknesses which I haven't been aware of until now?
4. Do people often make remarks which cut me to the quick?
5. Am I a sensitive and vulnerable person who cares what other people say and do?
6. How important are others' opinions to me?
7. How easily am I influenced by other people?
8. Do I easily adapt my opinion to that of others?
9. Am I emotionally in a difficult, unstable situation (e.g. separation, etc.)?
10. Do I experience others more quickly as energy suckers when I'm going through a stressful time?
11. Am I rather discontented with my life?
12. Do I often deceive myself - and then other people see through me?
13. Do I sometimes think I've put things behind me which still have to be resolved?

Take a look first at the questions you answered with 'sometimes' or 'very often.'

Analysis: Example A:

You answered Question 8 with "very much".

It's quite likely that you fall under the influence of others with exceptional ease, i.e. you're very inclined to let others take control of your life - which makes you 'easy prey' for psychovampires like the Snare Vampire. Now ask yourself if it matters to you that others rule your life. If it does, you need to work on yourself.

Analysis: Example B:

You answered Question 2 with 'very often'.

Because of your self-doubts it's quite possible that others see you as a 'Yes, but...' Vampire (see Chapter 3). At the same time you're a potential victim for all vampire types.

As a start, here are some suggestions as an aid to self-instruction which should in time lead to permanent 'immunization' against vampires.

- Think back to the basic conflict in your early life and read through the psychological mechanisms in Chapter 5 again.
- Consider the question of parental love and if you experienced it as conditional or unconditional.
- Be clear in your mind whether you feel your life is in your own hands or predominantly influenced by others.
- Make a list of the occasions in your personal past when you have felt drained and consider how you intend to act to better master such situations in future.

Am I a psychovampire to other people?

If you believe the legend from Transylvania, a vampire's bite will turn you into a vampire! This may be just an old saga handed down through generations but it does translate easily into modern day terms:

so many people try as hard as they can not to be the image of their parents and in most cases they fail completely to disconnect their own personality from the parental home because most of us never move beyond criticism and judgment and don't take a long hard and, above all, honest look at our own behaviour patterns. It is vital for you to arrive at a definition of your own self which can then positively shape your personal self-esteem. A state of so-called 'immunity' can only be achieved after a period of intensive self-reflection.

Exercise:

Imagine for a moment that, your partner, family, relatives, friends, and colleagues and superiors at work were asked to enumerate their personal psychovampires. Would you appear on their list perhaps - and if yes, how would you be classified? We've already looked at plenty of different vampire types. Could it be that you're regarded as energy sucking? Once you consider who or what you regard as exhausting and energy-consuming, it should be relatively easy to find out if others, for their part, also experience you in the same way.

Some examples of people who are experienced as psychovampires and would never have thought it possible:

- The mother who always has time for her children and is always there for them but never leaves them alone with their father for a week-end (a frequently heard line: "What will you eat, when I'm not there?"), is experienced as a psychovampire. Dad would probably welcome the chance of spending a few days alone with the kids, and does it really matter if they survive on spaghetti, McDonald's, etc.?
- The colleague who always gets his work done as soon as it comes in, whose desk is unfailingly tidy, whose E-mailbox is always up to date, etc., etc., is experienced as very exhausting by his co-workers.
- The friend who's (apparently) always in a good mood, never appears to have any problems and always smiles, is experienced by others, long term, as very exhausting.

- The boss who arrives early at the office every day - the first in the morning and the last to go in the evening - is as psychovampire for his employees. Everyone who comes later or goes earlier has a bad conscience or gives himself one. The fact that the boss is a workaholic, is divorced and only has his work to fill his life, is not taken into consideration at first glance.
- The housewife who often feels overwrought and can't help taking it out on her husband when the occasion arises ("It's fine for you, you have your career, I'm stuck with changing diapers"), must seem like a psychovampire to her partner.
- The man who's been asked the same question every day for the past 20 years: "How was your day?" and unfailingly offers the same reply, "Don't ask. Terrible, as usual", or the woman whose evening conversation topics seldom veer away from the kids, parents' evenings, the neighbours, etc., are experienced by their respective partners as psychovampires.

Any self-analysis requires a conscious awareness of how we *perceive ourselves and how others perceive us*. A very crucial but also very complex and challenging reflection will help us achieve this level of perception. It's a question of how I see myself and what emotions I release in others: sympathy, antipathy, eroticism, disinterest, interest, etc.

The following exercises have proved useful in practice:

1. What affect do you think you have on people when meeting them for the first time? Picture yourself entering a room in which a group of people is listening to someone making a speech. You're late and have to make your way through the rows, creating a disturbance and drawing everyone's attention. What feelings do you provoke as a person (leaving aside the fact that you arrived late)?
2. What in your opinion is the reaction of people you already know i.e. friends, relatives and colleagues? Are they glad to see you or do they suffer you out of a sense of politeness? Do these people feel good in your presence, emotionally secure, in good hands,

or more likely none of these? Do other people open up in your presence and do they also tell you spontaneously about their problems? Or does that seldom happen?

Now there's really only one way to sharpen your own perception of yourself – get some honest feedback from someone who's in a position to give some, a person who's a sound judge of character. As we have already discussed, there are astonishingly few people willing to give us a candid opinion of ourselves, and still fewer who are good judges of character. If you're lucky enough to meet some of this select of people in the course of your life, guard them like a treasure because they're vital to our personal development.

If we now assume that you've met one of this rare breed, the next step is to ask him how he perceives you. What are his immediate reactions when you enter a room? A concrete example will help illustrate this:

Brian (43 years old, cashier) is an elected member of a club committee which meets once a month. Brian, one of nine members, dominates the discussions with his constant interruptions; he generally manages to find something negative to say about everything, uses various manipulation techniques and needlessly prolongs the meeting. The other eight committee members, all there in an honorary capacity, have long since grown weary of these gatherings and often ask themselves why they bother to turn up at all. They've all had long discussions with each other about Brian but as yet no one has bucked up the courage to talk to him personally. They're all too afraid to confront him. A psychotherapist joins the club 'by chance' and, during a break at his first meeting, broaches the subject on everyone's mind. It soon becomes clear that all the other members are suffering but none of them dares to approach Brian and tell him what the problem is. At the next session Brian is absent for professional reasons, for which he duly apologizes profusely as he never misses out on these official events – who knows, decisions could be made against his will. The meeting in his absence is extremely productive; the atmosphere is wonderfully harmonious and everybody goes home buoyant with renewed enthusiasm and motivation. When

Brian is back at the next meeting it becomes clear to everyone after half an hour that the atmosphere is once again exceptionally tense, even aggressive at times, and that he's the cause of the trouble. The consequence is that many give up following the proceedings and doodle on their notepads. This would be just the right moment for Brian to get some honest feedback - and he gets some. One after the other – someone had to start the ball rolling – they make their feelings known to Brian, "When you were away the last week we had a very pleasant meeting, but no sooner are you back than the atmosphere changes. It's your fault. We don't want to go on working with you anymore. Either you fit in or you leave the committee." Brian is taken completely unawares and, for the first time in his life, is at a loss for words. To cut the story short: at the next meeting he's as if transformed. Of course, he can't help falling back into his 'old ways' from time to time, but he's never as extreme as before. It's worth noting here that the other board members couldn't remove Brian from the committee without the vote of all club members and this could only be obtained at a general meeting. But group pressure ("change or you cannot be a part of our group anymore") prevailed in the end. This was the first time that Brian received feedback and learned how others see him. For plausible reasons his wife wasn't able to give him any feedback during all their years of marriage while as a businessman he was automatically deprived of any employee feedback - at least theoretically; after all, which boss has so much self-confidence that he will openly invite criticism from his staff, or even encourage it?

If you have confirmed any suspicions about yourself as a possible psychovampire then a lot has already been achieved. Ask someone close to you if your self-perceived tendency to be a little tiring on occasions (it's probably better not the use the term "psychovampire"), also conforms to their perception of you. You can then discuss a possible course of action and this will definitely lead you to think more honestly about your own actions with the result that you'll hardly be recognized as a psychovampire in future.

Spare a thought too for the possibility that when you choose to slam other people from time to time, you're doing so to raise your own self-esteem. How does your self-esteem look these days? Do you need lots of reassurance from outside and do you sometimes exert pressure on others to get it?

Which boss has so much self-confidence that he will openly invite criticism from his staff, or even encourage it?

What now?

"There is no elevator to success. You have to take the stairs."
(Unknown)

Let's assume you've already become aware of the psychovampire phenomenon, have connected it to a few situations in your life and are feeling more relieved as a result. You've also received some inspirational ideas for future behaviour patterns. You may even start to change some things in your life - your strengths, which others might interpret as vampiric, can be toned down, leaving you time to work on your weaknesses.

Don't be mistaken into thinking that the authors of this book are no psychovampires themselves or that they are immune to psychovampires. In the process of writing this book, one of them outed himself as being an occasional Himalayas Vampire, while he himself was brought up in a family of Historical Monument Vampires. Does that make him a terrible person? For some, it might, for others his presence is barely perceptible. But it does suddenly seem reasonable and even logical that a person like the Himalayas Vampire, who knows no bounds in his activities and pushes others to the same limits, should react so allergically to Historical Monument Vampires, because Historical Monument Vampires are blockers in his view of the world. And it seems fairly clear why this particular alpine vampire became one in the first place – it was as an act of defiance, a counter-reaction to the Historical

Monument Vampires in the family who, in his eyes, go through life with the handbrake on.

Should you also have got wise to yourself and discovered that you embody one of vampire types described in this book, you're probably right now going back over your past life reviewing certain episodes and maybe even feeling remorse in some cases. Don't be too repentant though; look ahead instead and keep a watchful eye on your behaviour at work and in your private life. In all likelihood you'll identify one or more victims and figure out why you have difficulties with him or her. It's never too late to work on your own behaviour patterns or even overcome them.

It could also be that you're only a moderate, a not quite fully-fledged or even occasional vampire because the behaviour patterns described in the book are black-and-white descriptions, much simplified for the purposes of clarity. They leave plenty of room for grey tones in between, or for identifying multiple symptoms. One of the authors is acquainted with someone who combines Snare Vampire, Expert Vampire and Himalayas Vampire in one. After a five-year relationship marked by imbalance and suffering the victim broke off the friendship.

And please don't assume that the authors don't need to set limits for each other either. In an ideal world of human cooperation we're all well-balanced people - a balance between rational thinking and emotional control. Life's all about giving and taking and if we can create a true balance somewhere between the two, we wouldn't have to talk about vampirism any more. Consciously or not, people strive their whole life long to attain this balance which manifests itself in reasonable, deferential behaviour towards each other, in our private and working lives. In the end, it's all about tolerating each other's weaknesses. Everyone has weaknesses. To tolerate them and to help convert them into strengths is a worthy goal. Take a closer look at your tolerance levels.

We all go through different phases in life. In one of these phases we can be an absolute vampire to a friend. If the friendship is real and the friend is tolerant, this friendship will survive the bad phase, the victim will even be able to help the psychovampire and coach him through the bad times. This would also be an ideal state of affairs in interpersonal relationships. If we occasionally feel that our lives are being controlled by external circumstances which we cannot change, we should also use the opportunity to work on our tolerance levels. In some situations we can be as self-determined – i.e. not under threat as victims – as we want to be and still fall under the influence of others no matter how hard we fight against it. Self-determination requires a personal balance too; after all, someone who is too self-determined runs the risk of not being able to hold down a relationship! Today many partnerships fail to allow for conflict phases because both partners are too self-determined. In a society with a growing number of long-term singles, the ability, or the interest, required to deal with the differentness in our partner has been lost.

Having read this book and gone through a phase of intensive self-reflection you may just have the feeling that there are a lot of personal issues to be dealt with out there in the future. You might also have reached that disheartening state of self-awareness when you discover that your whole life has been one long story of being trapped in the role of victim, without ever realizing it. On this point, the authors can console you by confirming their own state of self-awareness - and that they have learnt to laugh about it!

Vampire immunization is a lifelong project. It's like working out: you only get better if you train every day. There's no life free of vampires but you can work daily on your balanced self-determination. It's worth it! After all, it's your life!

Think ahead, be ahead.

(Antoine de Saint-Exupery)

Would you like to share your story with us? We'd love to read it. For more information contact the authors at: www.psychovampire.com or www.interculturalcenter.com

hamid@peseschkian.com
C@interculturalcenter.com

"Reflection is looking in so you can look out with a broader, bigger, and more accurate perspective."
— Mick Ukleja and Robert Lorber

Printed in the United States
By Bookmasters